# BREAKING BREAD WITH

M000289217

## JERRY ELLIS

Author of the Pulitzer Prize-nominated book
WALKING THE TRAIL, ONE MAN'S
JOURNEY ALONG THE CHEROKEE TRAIL
OF TEARS

Jerry Ellis

1714 A Smith Gap Road NW

Fort Payne, Alabama 35968

Wild Indian Productions ISBN 978-0-985151-4-1

# AUTHOR

Jerry Ellis, the author of nine books, was the first person in the modern world to walk the 900-mile route of the Cherokee Trail of Tears, and his resulting nonfiction book, Walking the Trail, was nominated by Delacrote Press for a Pulitzer Prize and a National Book Award. He has lectured, via storytelling performances, about the Cherokee and his walk in Asia, Africa, Europe, and the USA. He has been published in The New York Times, had numerous short stories published, and five plays produced. He lives in both Rome, Italy and in Fort Payne, Alabama.

"Writing, at its best, is a **lonely** life. ... He grows in public stature as he sheds his **loneliness** and often his work deteriorates. For he does his work alone and if he is a good enough writer he must face eternity, or the lack of it, each day." Ernest Hemingway

# For Melissa

I live alone at Tanager House on 60 wooded acres in NE Alabama. My late wife and soulmate, Debi, must receive most of the creative credit for designing our home like an Italian villa. A massive six foot deep fountain flows in the center of the house, the statue of a goddess adorning a pedestal with water cascading from her feet, as though eternal life itself lives in Woman as well as Water, the two having been ONE since the beginning of Time Divine, Praise to the Great Mystery.

Being a very private person by choice, save in my stories, books, and seminars, I invite only the most select humans to visit me and especially for overnight. I recently invited into my home, Melissa Wilson, for a couple of days. Her mind and spirit are as layered as the Earth itself. She is an Adventurer, a Dare Devil, deep thinker, a law enforcement officer, a mother, a grandmother, a daughter, a sister, a Spiritual Warrior, and one of the most loving and generous friends introduced to me many years ago by the Great Mystery. She once read about a long Trail I, in desperation, walked to find myself, dropping breadcrumbs along the way for others who were as hungry as I was.

When Melissa, Mel, visited me, I took her to many of our area's Cherokee historic sites and even to look for ancient stone Native American artifacts, her eyes becoming those of a child, perhaps a starling contrast to her eyes when she worked as a tower gunner at a prison in California. We walked in a creek to seek the artifacts and the water rushing over her feet was the same Divine Water that flows from the goddess in the fountain at Tanager House. It's TRUE, Water ALWAYS seeks its own level and in the creek that joyous day, I saw Mel rise up as if baptized by Wonder, her Wonder cleansing my soul in ways she might not have guessed.

I dedicate Breaking Bread with Misfits, Spiritual Food for the Hungry, to Mel. This announcement may or may not be but a mere bursting bubble in a remote mountain stream to you, but for me it is the eternal Fountain of Friendship, where humankind drinks from the glass that is never half empty but forever overflowing, at least for a while, on our short Earthly bread-crumb feasting journey. I love you, Mel, my dear Friend. THANK YOU for all your generous and kind support over the years.

I've heard rumors about the Magical Loving Beings called Mothers and I once had ONE. My first memory of my mother was when I stood all ALONE in my baby bed, my fingers tight around the bed railing as I cried, "Mama, mama!" She soon loomed out the mysterious nowhere with her tender smile and took me into her securing arms.

When my heart was broken for the first romantic time, at 17, I confided in her late one night. She listened daring not to interrupt and finally said, as she hugged me, "I'm so sorry, honey. You hurt is my hurt."

When I once returned home, which I did again, and again, from thumbing America and Mexico, she asked me to help gather large stones, twice as big as basketballs to create a border around flowerbeds.

She chose the prized stones in our woods and said, "I like those that looked like something happened to them." She only had an eight-grade education but was as gracious as the Queen she was. Whenever I was sick as a child, she stayed up all night sitting with me to keep a wet washcloth on my forehead, the same she did when I was once drunk in adulthood, nursing me back to sanity without daring to cast blame or guilt. When I walked the Trail for 900 miles, she appeared at night, as I arrived home, as a white ghost walking the driveway as she paced back and forth.in her silk nightgown.

When she fell from the bed on Christmas day 4 years ago and injured her head, bleeding on the brain, she was soon bound for Glory Land in a nursing home. She was 96. The last time I saw her she was in a wheelchair.

"I saw your daddy today," she said. My father had died many years ago. I recalled how he always kissed her when he left for work. "I drove to see him in a pickup truck."

"Mama," I said, "can you still sing sacred harp?"

Sacred harp, also called four note, performs without music, save for the music of the human voice. Her eyes searched mine as if to find an answer. She watched my hand seemingly come of the mysterious unknown to touch her forehead.

"It's okay, Mama," I said. "It's hard to remember everything."

There in her wheel chair pickup truck, shifting gears, she sang," I got a home in Glory Land that outshines the sun."

Shine on, Mama! As I pray your Light yet shines on, however humble and dim, from me. I love you for all your kindness and mercy, and especially when I was once lost and you yet believed in me.

When I toured four countries in Asia on a speaking tour, I spoke to all grades at Hong Kong School International. I had just told a group of first graders about Cherokee myths, that a screech owl hooting in the night was always a witch coming to kidnap children as they slept. "The only way to stop the witch," I said, "is to hurry a boom over the threshold of the front door."

A terrified girl shot her hand into the air as her eyes begged. "Mr. Ellis," her voice trembled, "we only have a vacuum cleaner in our home."

When I was seventeen, I stood on the New Jersey Turnpike, and held the same piece of cardboard I had used to run away from Alabama. Now, however, the words New York faced me. The side presented to passing traffic said Chattanooga, Tennessee.

A New Jersey State Police car, going the opposite direction, slowed and the driver glowered. His speaker barked: "Get off the turnpike or you will be arrested."

I picked up my bag and started back toward the turnpike entrance booth. I continued to hold my Chattanooga sign to the motorists. I wore my customary tight T-shirt, and I had made certain that morning that all my clothes were clean and ironed.

A Volkswagen Beetle approached, and its squeaking brakes were the sound of success to a now experienced hitchhiker like me. I could make out that the two men in the car sported dark shades, wore jet-black hair and were huge.

The passenger opened the door, got out and pulled his seat forward to let me in. He was big, all right. I felt like a hill next to a mountain.

"Good morning," he flashed his white teeth and appeared to be two or three years older than I.

"Thanks for stopping," I said and hopped in. "You guys came at a good time. The cops just gave me a warning."

"Happy we could help," said the driver. While in New York I had become so fascinated with the natives' accents that I began to guess which of the five boroughs people were from. I was usually wrong.

"You guys from Brooklyn?" I said.

As the car moved on they both glanced my way and smiled. "That's right," said the passenger. "Are you from Yonkers?"

I glanced at the guy in the rear-view mirror to make sure he was joking. "Yeah," I said. "But I've been trying to learn an Alabama accent." The men seemed eerily familiar. "Are you actors?"

"Oh, we act sometimes," said the passenger. "But we don't get paid for it."

"Do you know Dave Collier in Chattanooga?" said the driver.

I did know Collier. He owned and operated a gym there, and had sponsored recent weightlifting and physique contests.

"Wait a minute," I said, as clues flew together, "who are you guys?"

"I'm Joe Abbenda," said the driver.

"No way," the words leaped from me. I had seen Joe on the television show *To Tell the Truth* and in bodybuilding magazines. A history teacher, he had won major physique titles, including Mr. Universe.

"My friend here is Dennis Tinerino," said Joe. I had seen Dennis in the magazines as well, and I sat staring in near disbelief.

"*Very* wild," I finally managed to say.

"I won the Mr. Teenage America Contest last week," said Dennis. "We're on the way now to York, Pennsylvania with pictures for the editors to decide which one they want to put on the cover of *Strength and Health* or *Muscular Development*."

"We could see that you lift weights," said Joe. "That's why we stopped for you. People in the iron game have to stick together."

"I met Sig Klein," I announced, proud to be part of the inner circle. "I went to his gym in Manhattan." Sig was one of the most famous strongmen on Earth.

"We know Sig," said Joe. "Did he offer you a cigar?"

I was already aching to tell the kids back home about meeting Joe and Dennis, but I was dying to tell the story to my boss, John. He would love this profound coincidence as much as he loved his tabloids, where he had read that rats as big as dogs roamed the New York subway tunnels.

"York is not much out of your way," said Dennis. "Why don't you come with us and have lunch there?"

It was one thing to join the Hell's Angels on their trip to south Florida, but now to be invited to York with Mr. Universe and Mr. Teenage America was another. Not only was it becoming clear that the road could fill with wonderful surprises, I was almost starting to expect it.


I have discovered a new and exciting way to promote my books! I stand on Interstate 59 in Alabama and hold a HUGE sign. I have sold several copies to Highway Patrolmen.


Living in New Orleans for eight years, I encountered many exotic and compelling characters. Susan, from New York, who was a painter, and she was good, even sold enough Art to support herself and her daughter.

She invited me to her home one summer night and she mixed two gin and tonics, which we started to consume on her front porch swing, magnolias blooming in her yard, a rusty antique iron gate that squeaked before her entrance. A magnolia tree bloomed lush whites and a plastic purple necklace of Mardi Gras beads dangled from the tree's limb. The Saint Charles street car rang in the distance.

"May I tell you a secret?" she rattled the cold cubes in her glass and her feet stopped the swing. Wind made her long hair dance.

I simply nodded.

"A couple of years ago," she began, "I lost a lover. One I thought was my soulmate. He left me for another woman. A bartender on Bourbon Street."

She bit her lip. Looked away from my eyes. Then back to them as she took a deep breath. "I cried uncontrollably for two days." Her nervous laugh saddened my heart. She reached into her pocket, her black pants strained with red and blue Artist paint. Her hand hid in her pocket.

"Do I really want to do this?" she seemed to ask herself.

She took a breath. I sipped my gin and tonic, my gaze tender to her troubled eyes.

"I filled this with some of my tears," she found the courage. She pulled a polished silver antique thimble from her pocket and handed it to me. "I placed the tears in the freezer." She rattled gently her glass. "One of the cubes is made of tears. I promised myself I would use it when I was again able to smile." The streetcar rang in the distance. "I guess you think I'm pretty strange?" Her voice had become timid, and that made her even more endearing. I had seen many of her paintings and they ranged from realistic for the New Orleans tourists as they depicted the French Quarter with black wrought iron balconies and green and yellow banana trees with little green frogs perched atop them with the great Mississippi River flowing in the background, to more personal Art that reminded me of Picasso.

"I think," I said, "that you found a way to see beauty even in sorrow."

She smiled. I raised my glass and dinged the rim against her glass. It will forever ring out in the universe of my heart.

When I first met an elderly priest several years ago in Rome, I didn't have a clue what I was in store for. It was early one Sunday morning in Trastevere where I lived, bordered by the Tiber River. I was the only customer at an outdoor café, and the old priest walked very slowly down the alley. When we made eye contact, I was just too intrigued to let him pass.

"Good morning," I said in Italian. He said the same but he was clearly an American. "Could I buy you a coffee?" He took a chair. "Where are you headed?" I asked. "To see a foot," he chuckled. "A very old foot."

I bit: "What do you mean?"

"It's a relic," he said, "the foot of one of my saints, Teresa of Avila. She was a Carmelite nun, a mystic, a healer and a spiritual advisor. Her foot's in the church just up there, the Church of Santa Maria della Scala. If you ever want to see it just ask the custodian. They're happy to show it."

Okay, this was one of the more interesting introductions to a stranger I had ever had. He said he went by the name Jake but his given name was Peter Jacobs.

"What do you do?" He said. I told him my profession and our coffee arrived. "Oh, I always get along with writers really well," he continued. "Norman Mailer is a good friend of mine. I married him to one of his wives. I'm also close to the Hemmingway family. Woody Allen is a friend. Yoko I guess is more of a painter than a writer but…Oh, I know a boatful of writers. I used to hang out at the Lion's Den in the Village. Damned shame they closed it down." He sipped his coffee. "What kind of stuff you write?"

"Wait," I said, "never mind about me. You're really friends with all those people?"

"Sure," he said. "I have a lot of interesting friends. Some are royalty and others are just what the insensitive world brands as riff-raff. I used to visit the Prince of Monaco before Grace Kelly died. When she passed I conducted her eulogy. We used to have good times sitting around the pool with the king of Spain and—

I couldn't take it anymore. "Jake," I said, "this is all just bullshit, right?"

He chuckled as if his spirit was as free as the wind.

"Sounds like it, doesn't it?" He finished his coffee and

stood. "Not smart to keep a saint waiting," he added, "even if it is just her foot." He started on his merry way but then turned. "I have coffee every morning just around the bend there if you ever want to join me."

I watched Father Jake slowly wobble down the alley toward the sacred relic or at least that's where he claimed he was going. For all I knew he was headed to the hospital across from Quando in Roma to tell some whoppers in the mental ward. Within the hour I was on the Internet Googling Peter Jacobs aka "Jake." Son-of-a-bitch, the guy was real and had done far more than I had given him a chance to brag about. He grew up in New York's neighborhood known as Hell's Kitchen and as a priest taught the poor and disenfranchised in Harlem. Pope John Paul had been so impressed by Jake's dedication to God and the Catholic Church that the pope arrived by private motorcade to visit Jake at the school, the media onto the story like a hound dog onto a rabbit. There was, however, a small snag. Jake wasn't there. He was going about his Godly business of caring for addicts and prostitutes on the lower East Side.

I played dumb to all the extensive information I had uncovered about Jake when I met him for coffee the next morning. He didn't look surprised in the least to find me waiting for him and pulled up a chair as if he had been doing so for years with me.

"How was the foot yesterday?" I asked.

"Pretty dried out after so many years," he said. "You really should go see it. Since you have done so much walking in your life you'd value it more than some." He looked up to return the wave of a woman watering potted plants in her second floor window.

"Know who Tyrone Powers was?" He said.

"Sure," I said, "he was a mega movie star back in the thirties and forties."

"That's his daughter watering the plants," said Jake. "I got my fill of water decades ago when I joined the Navy." He chuckled and touched his black cap with the words **New York Yankees** sewn into it. "We used to tuck our condoms right here out of sight in our sailor's cap when we had shore leave. Oh, yeah, I was young once upon a time." He gave me an odd look.

"You're not like most writers," He continued. "They'd rather talk about themselves than listen." "I'm worse than all of them put together," I said. "I just haven't been able to get a word in edgewise with you, Jake."

He gave that already famous little chuckle and continued. "I've always been a thorn in the Catholic Church. I've taken confessions in bars, at street corners and just about anywhere. Done a lot work in prisons, too. Saint Francis of Assisi is my principal saint. I give everything to the poor and needy like he did. A person doesn't really need much to be happy he just gets caught up in the world and thinks he needs a bunch of stuff."

The next several weeks I met Jake almost every morning for coffee and he became my friend. When he flew to New York for a week to see his heart doctor and visit friends I took in his mail and made sure his apartment was okay. He lived like a monk in the humble flat with only a bed, couch and a couple of chairs, no paintings on the wall—just a cross hung here and there. He did, however, collect old books and magazines and they were stacked several feet high in one corner of the living room. A web, with a spider unlike I had ever seen, stretched from the top of the stack to the ceiling. I started to roll up a copy of *Time* to knock it down. But I decided against it in case Jake had come to care for it in some oddly sacred manner that holy men are said to do.

It was a whole year after meeting Jake that he finally confessed to me one morning over coffee what I had already learned. "We all make mistakes," he started, "and I made a big one a couple of years back. A man in the United States offered to give big money to one of charities if I would introduce him to powerful people inside the Vatican. I did and it turned out he was using that connection to launder millions of dollars. He went to prison and I got five years' probation. I knew I was innocent but even one of oldest and dearest friends doubted me. It was Walter Cronkite and I had been his spiritual advisor for decades. He finally apologized to me for having suspicions and I forgave him like we all should forgive each other. But before Walter came back to me I lived a daily sorrow deep in my heart." Jake placed his hand on my knee. "Always remember to talk openly with a friend before a minor cut festers into an ugly sore."

"I'll remember," I said.

The last time I saw Jake was the day after he phoned me in Rome to say that Walter Cronkite's daughter was staying with him. He asked if I wanted to meet her the next morning. I arrived at the café and foolishly expected her to be elegantly dressed and sophisticated. But she was plump and wore sloppy wrinkled clothes. Her boyfriend carried a guitar.

"Something wrong?" I asked Jake who wore dark shades and wasn't his talkative self.

"I got bitten in the night," he removed his shades to reveal a black spot the size of a pea in the corner of his eye. "I'm taking it to a lab to determine what kind of spider it is. I don't feel so good." He pulled a vial from his shirt pocket that housed the creature that bit him.

That was the last time I saw Jake. He didn't die from the bite but from a heart attack in Rome. On the wall of the café where he and I had met so many times for coffee the owner had hung Jake's obituary. Among those who came to his funeral were Walter Cronkite and Yoko Ono.


THEY have come, many of THEM, over the years. Uninvited. Knocking on the door of my beloved parents, both now buried on the other side of Highway 11 in north Fort Payne, Alabama in the cemetery across from Dekalb County's second largest Indian mound built over 1,000 years ago, in the bend by Will's Creek, that stretch of road called Dead Man's Curve.

THESE people who knocked, wanting to know if a certain author lived there. "Would just like to meet him, if he's here?" I always came outside, my mother proud, my father hiding his own pride behind a subtle lightning-fast grin.

"Happy to meet you," I always shook their hands, the actor in me able to hide the sense of intrusion. However, one day my guard dropped, stripped naked.

A man about my age now, wearing overalls, those brass buttons faded by sun and hard-work sweat, said: "Mr. Ellis I'm

very sorry to bother you but my grandson so wants to meet you."
His redhaired grandson pondered my eyes.

"I..I..I..loved your book, sir." He lifted the book from his side. "I..I...I read it three times." He extended the book. "Any..any chance you would sign it, sir?"

I fought tears, for whose life itself has not stuttered along the way, not in words but in his long-short earthly journey? The grandfather pulled a long yellow pencil from his faded-blue overalls.

"He..he...sharpened it for you," the ten-year-old boy was so proud of his grandfather. But perhaps not as rightly proud as his grandfather was of the boy.

I signed his book and said to the boy, "I have something I was saving just for YOU." His eyes grew bigger than Will's Creek and the Indian mound there.

I returned moments later with my fist around a kind of key, the one to my often-protected heart. "Hold out your hand," I suggested.

His hand and mine both trembled a bit. I opened my fingers to drop two inches, an arrowhead, the boy feeling the Ancient Ones.

"Mine?" he gasped.

"Just for YOU," I answered.

His grandfather placed his big hand on the boy's head. "Wait in the car, son."

The boy did as told, the car door creaking.

"That means more to him than you will ever know," said the man. "To me as well."

We shook hands and he got into the car, backed up and drove down my parents' drive, into my soul, as the boy waved and held up the book, the arrowhead between the lines written in the story of our lives.


The sun inches its brilliant and ancient path my way over beautiful Lookout Mountain. The wind howls and the bamboo patch beneath my second floor office, where I am now, quivers its evergreen leaves. Those leaves whisper my father, who dropped dead over 20 years ago doing what he loved: He was working in his garden, planting whip-poor-will peas, one that is site of an Indian village over 8,000 years old. How do I know its age? I have been studying archaeology for decades and have found stone artifacts there and not arrowheads only. But back to my father in the bamboo leaves. He started the bamboo patch at our home over 50 years ago, got a couple from my mother's brother in Chattanooga. It took years for the bamboo to spread its determined roots and grow a true thick patch of cane. While some grew skyward 15-20 feet, I was disappointed that their shafts were only as big around as a quarter. Decades later, however, they are now almost as big around as my wrists. Know what? Those bamboos thrive in an ancient road, one that began as an animal trail. It became the Bellfonte Gap Road, traveled by the Creek Indians up over Sand Mountain through a natural gap onto the Tennessee River. When the Cherokee pushed the Creek south and settled here, they used the Gap Road, its ruts very clearly seen and documented that 90 Cherokee departed there for Indian Territory before most of our tribe was rounded up at Fort Payne, where I am now, in 1838 for the Trail of Tears. That Gap Road comes through my mother's property at the foot of the hill where I live. It's twenty feet from where my father gave up the Ghost while working in the garden. His passing was the worst day of my life, but praise to the Great Mystery, my father lives on the bamboo just beneath me now as I respectfully reach out to you just before dawn. The bending strong bamboo's green leaves whisper a song to me. They sing of love, tenderness, and memories of an old man who I once saw plow that garden with a mule. While the bamboo in the wind sings my father's songs I wonder what songs trees sing that I have not yet heard?

We baptize ourselves in different ways and the Cherokee traditionally would "go to water" each morning, washing their faces in a stream or spring to wash away any of the night's darkness, witches capable of haunting one's dreams.

Today I "went to water" at one of my favorite creeks not only to feel better bonded with Nature, where at this creek I have beheld otters, deer, wild pigs and my Spirit bird, the crane, turtles, and fish swimming like silver shining, but, as you guessed, to look for ancient stone Indian artifacts. The Ancient Ones are often so loving, it seems, and certainly generous to me as they reveal their treasures. Smile or even laugh but some impassioned artifact seekers strongly believe that certain artifacts will only appear to particular people. It's okay to say, "That's nonsense, just luck." The Ancient Ones don't care what you say or think, but in the same breath they may hide their treasures from non-believers. Our world is rich with wondrous events, and I pray your heart overflows with them.

I wouldn't reveal sentimentality if I didn't believe that it also relates to YOU and especially if you grew up in my beloved South. My grandfather walked 300 miles from East Tennessee, a village called Shady Valley near the Eastern Band of Cherokee at Cherokee, NC, to the mountains of NE Alabama. He made the walk with an ox in the late 1800s. He was not only a stone mason, he had the last water powered grist mill in my county and was the last man to go to town, Fort Payne, in a buggy pulled by a mule. He wrote poetry, played the fiddle, and sang Sacred Harp. He farmed, and hunted and sold ginseng to help support his 12 children. A tender, strong and loving man, he kept the child alive in his soul and at a stream near his home, with two hand-dug wells, created a little water driven hammer that rose and fell to pound a stone, Nature's clock to speak of sacred time, passing beat by beat in the hammer hitting the stone.

When he died at 85, his body in a hearse arrived at his home, where dozens of his family members watched outside as the hearse drove down the long dirt road to deliver his body for display in the fireplace room. His wife, upon seeing the hearse, threw her hands toward the sky as she screamed crying. He was a brown-skinned man, his Native American heritage apparent in skin and sensitivity. When I was a boy, he wrote me a very personal letter, confiding that when he was a teen he was once walking alone when, "The spirit of the Lord came to me in the wind, a wind so strong that it lifted me above the trees into the arms of God. If you ask, the Lord will lift you into the sky." I'm still flying, Grandpa, and I daily hear the Earth talking to me, your water hammer hitting the stone in the creek, mapping my Earthly journey with your love and kindness. Sometimes, even to this day, I call crows with my mouth and hand as you taught me when I was a child. The crows and I fly together, with you nearby.

My long-time friend, Dan, who grew up in windblown Oklahoma, was brilliant and got his masters at Yale. He went to a Cadillac dealer in OKC. The owner of the dealership was a friend to Dan's brother. Dan, an accomplished author, received the red carpet. He found a Caddy he liked and the dealer said, "Take it for a test drive. Make sure you are comfortable in it. Take your time."

"I'll do that," said Dan, receiving the car keys. "Thank you."

Dan pulled from the car lot for the test drive. He drove through downtown OKC and hit the interstate.

He continued the test drive westward past rolling tumbleweeds and pumping oil derricks into Tennessee and onto North Carolina.

Dan's brother had to fly from Oklahoma to NC to get the car and Dan back to OKC. The test drive, however, proved worthy. Dan decided a Lincoln Continental suited him better.

Yes, I have met a few characters on my JOURNEY. I suppose some of those characters could say the same about me.

Sometimes I talk to myself, other people, the written page, birds, and even flowers. Yesterday, I sat on the ground by the spring's first yellow crocus to bloom. I was about to speak to it, when it whispered.

"I knew you'd be coming around. From down in the winter's earth, I heard you walk by me many times. I felt your joy. Your sorrow. Your dreams and memories. I'm happy you are here near me now. You can touch me if you want. You are a gentle soul. I have bloomed for YOU. Do you know why?"

My fingertips brushed the flower as I once touched the silky hair of my late wife, Debi. "Yes," I answered. "I know why you bloomed for me."

"I will be gone in just a couple of days. Keep me near your heart to draw strength and beauty when I have faded away. I'll see you again, later on down the road."

In 2006, I wrote a poem for my late wife of 28 years, Debi. "Do you know what became of the poem?" I asked years after I had written it.

Debi eyed me as only she could do. "It's with me," she said.

"What do you mean?"

"I carry the poem folded in my purse," she said.

"How long have you been carrying it?" I asked.

"Since you gave it to me," she said.

"That was many years ago," I said. She grinned and nodded.

The poem:

## Sounds Like You

When I awake long before dawn and hear the goddess fountain, overflowing with ancient and constant promises of beauty with life-giving rain, undiscovered waterfalls, endless streams and rivers and mysterious seas, her whispers pale when I hear you breathe beside me in bed. You are the day's true song, assuring me that the human soul runs deeper than all the waters of the world.

While the sun has yet to arrive and I sit in my office overlooking the vast beauty and sorrows of my life, NPR rattles the radio and the fireplace blazes its gentle hiss. But the only sound that really matters is the music of the creaking stairs, when you climb from your slumber to enter the room, a promise that our love is as constant as the morning light.

The rattling ice in your glass filled with Coke is not some cold island where the wind howls forever. It is a sunny shore where your footprints always lead me to your eyes and lips, the gleam and smile there always a lighthouse after the long dark night.

Even the opening of your plastic Coke bottle with its tiny explosion seems as vital to Nature as the calls of birds or their pecking on the porch pole's bird suet. When you speak your first words of the day, the very sound of your voice makes Lookout Mountain listen. For without you, it would disappear just as my heart would vanish.

When your fingers tap the keyboard of your computer, they are sounds of your soul seeking to gift the less fortunate world with treasures to lift them from their pains that they too might fly beside you. You inspire me to soar simply when I look upon you, knowing you are near.

When you play your piano in the cottage and sing, such beautiful sounds reveal you like only the moans of your seductive body can tell when we make love. It is then that all the other sounds come together and make me melt into the humility and joy to hear my own breath and be grateful for the next beat of my heart.

When you are away from me in Italy, I am deaf, pretending to listen to others as I nod or smile but I can only see their lips moving, just as I can only image what the wind or the song of a bird is really like. I am lost in memory of your face and every little thing about you, waiting for the stairs to creak again as you and only you can enter the most treasured and private room of that home within. (Valentine's Day—2006)


After all these decades (DECADES? Oh, my!), I still see the old man's sparkling eyes and remember like yesterday what he told me, his smile worth a million bucks. We were sitting in a coffee spot in San Francisco's North Beach, where drifters and famous artists once gathered. My own humble reputation yet floated in the womb of dreams, aspiring ambitions.

But WHAT did that old man tell me, his white beard as long and bushy as that of Rip Van Winkle?

He leaned toward me, his wrinkled face glowing, and said, "Oh, I remember it so well."

I bit. "Remember what?" I said.

His fingers played in his beard as though it became one with his hand. "I remember when tree holes were filled with little toys. For boys who knew how to climb limbs. You climbed trees when you were a boy didn't you?"

I was both amused and startled, his words pulling me closer. "Yes, sir," I said. "I did at that. How did you know?"

His grin was subtle, as if we shared a secret. "I see the toys in your eyes. Once they are there they rarely go away."


The elder had lived alone the past five years since her husband of forty-five years had passed. In thick woods, she savored the log cabin she had inherited from her parents built by her great grandparents in the mountains. She knew the woods like the back of her wrinkled hand and she had heard many birds sing. One day, at sunrise, she heard a song she had never heard before, what seemed like the combination of an owl hooting and a whip-poor-will calling out, though it sometimes reminded her of a joyful crow or a playful blue jay.

Each time she wandered in the woods toward the song, she felt she was, at last, about to find its rare source and see the bird. It vanished in the shifting wind. Anticipation replaced by disappointment, she reckoned, was one thing you could always count on in life, not denying its many wonders. Private wonders she kept to herself.

Sometimes she heard the song in the night, awakening her as her husband did from time to time, as he had eased his hand into her long hair at the neck, his breathing a kind of song.

It was almost dusk with the sun setting over Sand Mountain, when she walked the woods to behold the treasured source of the song. The bird was fifty feet from the ground up in a towering oak. It was a hole in the tree, the wind whistling its magical song. Long after darkness fell, and the moon rose, she stood as if under a spell looking up at the hole-bird, the wind enriching the night forest with its golden and mysterious sounds.

She struggled to drag her rocking chair from her front porch and into the woods. There she sat most of the day and even into the night, hoping the wind would come.

"Sing to me," her whispers pleaded. The times between songs, she reckoned, is not up to us. But sooner, or later the wind always returned with its songs born in the mysterious and magical hole in the tree.

A week later, as she rested in bed, a thunderstorm blew through the night as rain poured, her ears seeking the song, even among loud booms. The next morning, though the wind blew, the song was silent, like the lips of the dead.

She hurried into her robe and didn't bother with shoes, as she rushed into the woods. She soon froze, her old eyes staring in near disbelief. The giant oak stretched out on the earth, some of its limbs broken, while others had pierced the ground. The huge ball of roots was like a bundle of snakes trapped in earth.

She forced herself to step closer. She bent over the hole in the tree. Her shaky fingers lifted from her side and tenderly touched the hole-bird.

"I am so sorry," she whispered. She took a deep breath, a sigh rising from her soul. "Maybe more for me than you," her confession startled her, weighing on her aging heart.

It took her two days with a handsaw to cut through the oak, sweat dripping from her brow. She was not as strong as she had once been and it took three days to drag the saved part of the tree to her yard and just a few feet from her front porch. Dragging the rocking chair back to the porch was easy, compared to moving the bird.

She used a shovel to dig a hole in the ground and somehow managed to drag and push the treasured part of the tree upright. When the wind blew, the hole-bird didn't make the same sounds as before. No, its songs were even sweeter and more beautiful now. Yet, sometimes, sadder, like a bird seeking another bird, one too far away to hear the call.

When my stepson was about 10 years old, I took him to hunt for Easter eggs, in the woods around my home in the mountains of NE Alabama. He was intrigued but puzzled. Why was I carrying a rifle?

We came to a spot in the woods, where 12 eggs dangled from strings three feet from tree limbs. He had never shot a gun before and I went first, aimed the rifle and fired. One of the eggs exploded, yellow flashing against the blue sky.

I handed him the gun after a few choice instructions, like, "Don't shoot me."

He took a deep breath, raised the rifle, aimed and BOOM, more liquid painting the blue sky yellow. That was over 20 years ago and some of that yellow yet paints my heart happy. Not for the shooting of the eggs as much as for this California city boy's smile. Sometimes, things become holy in ways we have not yet imagined.


Funny, what we remember years later isn't it? What sticks with us, and how in time we reflect upon it. I once went to New York to visit and do some "business" with key players at Random

House. We all went to a fancy restaurant. It was fun, "business" whispered between the lines.

One night Emily, my editor, the executive editor, took me to a restaurant, where agents and other editors took their writers. Everyone was checking out the others. WHO is SHE? WHO is HE? Oh, my, is that who I think it is. Not so much pretention as intense human curiosity. And competition. I was happy and amazed that I was even there at all.

Emily, who had flown from New York to Fort Payne, Alabama to see how I lived and meet my parents, do video of me for the sales reps for my book, Walking the Trail, One Man's Journey Along the Cherokee Trail of Tears, was beyond lovely. Modest. Loving. Kind. Smart as a whip.

She said two things that standout now with glimmering clarity.

"I think my writing is rather simple and to the point," I said.

She said, "In simplicity sometimes brilliances shines through. Hemingway wrote that way."

"My agent thinks some of my work is too personal." My words hit a nerve.

"People say that when they are afraid of better knowing themselves," her voice both firm and tender. She was wiser than I was.

When Emily visited my parents and me in Alabama, we had breakfast, made by beloved mother, downhome and gracious. Emily was mesmerized to watch mother make biscuits, a thumbnail of white flour smeared on my mother's nose. It was the first time Emily ever ate biscuits and gravy, an exotic, if not strange, dish to her. There are many ways to break bread with misfits and eating biscuits is one. I yet taste the sacred bread of that morning with Emily and after all these many years, it continues to nourish my soul.

Emily decided to leave the publishing business and to get married to start a family. She phoned all her writers to tell them.

"I was fine telling the others," she said to me on the phone, "until it came to you." She fought tears.

"Everything is going to be okay," I tried to hide my own tears.

When she had her first child, Olivia, my mother quilted her a baby blanket. Emily mailed us a photo of her on the blanket with Oliva as Emily read a book to her. I am not sure, even to this day, if my tears were of sorrow or joy. Perhaps like the multicolored quilt my mother had made for Emily's daughter, my deep emotions were a tapestry of both.

"What counts most, as I look back over the years, are not my accomplishments but rather the friends who worked with me as partners in these accomplishments. The funny thing about it all is that the quality and quantity of those accomplishments are fuzzy and unimportant in my mind, while the friendships remain crystal clear in my memory." Mark Twain

Back in the 50s, we left Fort Payne, Alabama and lived in Cleveland, TN for a while so my father, a carpenter, could find work. The ice plant was only a quarter mile away, and when I was

12, at my request, my hammer-sure-shot dad built me a snowball wagon. We found scrap lumber and old but good bicycle tires. I colored the pushcart bright white and painted the image of a snowball in a cone on both sides of my new business. I added, "5 cents" and "10 cents."

Daddy "loaned" me money to buy a metal ice scraper and cherry and grape concentrate that was to be mixed with sugar and water. Paper straws.

My first day, pushing my new cart to the ice plant, the metal ice scraper, tied to the side of the sure-to-make-it business, rattled, just as I envisioned coins would soon jingle-jangle in my jeans' needy and ambitious pocket.

I got a BIG block of ice. For 50 cents. Even as a kid, I believed in the American Dream. Work hard. Make it.

Pushing the cart around the neighborhood, I yelled out in my Alabama accent, "Snowballs! Snowballs! Five and ten cents!"

To see a kid running toward me excited me. To behold several kids dashing my way THRILLED me. When a man gave me my first "tip," I had never heard the word before.

Some summer days, I pushed that snowball wagon for miles, the ice scraper rattling against the side of the wooden wagon with coins turning cartwheels in my pocket.

Every day, when my father got home, sweaty, tired, and dirty, he'd say, "Did you roll'em today, son?"

I'd usually answer, "Sure did, Pa."

"How much did you make?" He had grown up poor.

I was proud on the days that I had scraped the block of ice to the bottom One day I made a WHOLE 5 bucks, and I couldn't wait for daddy to get home from work.

That old scratched and dinted ice scraper now hangs in our Alabama barn, one daddy built all by himself. The scraper is only a few feet from my younger sister's leather horse reins. She got the horse, Princess, when it was a colt and Princess lived for almost 20 years. Before we buried her in the pasture, dragged to the hole in the ground by daddy's tractor.

I just want you to know, Pa, in the Empire of the Great Mystery, that I still "roll'em."

"Snowballs! Snowballs! Five and ten cents!"

The moment you conceived inside your beloved mother, a spark flashed. Honor your mother and father and the Devine, walking with grace, dignity, strength, and compassion. Hear the tender thunder every time your heart beats.

Today in Rome, Italy!

It's a national holiday here and the streets are jumping with festive folks strolling, laughing, talking, sipping wine, and--of course--enjoying the national sport of Italy: Flirting! I am busy taking notes of who is doing the best at it and, oh, my, many are in line for the World Cup of Flirting. Those that are the most polished at the Game do it in the most subtle ways. A kiss blown across an outdoor cafe in one's very breath. Yes, the air here today is sweet and inviting. Now please excuse me while I wander on to write down the scores of many more contestants.

Some folks, bless their hearts, are walking yawns. Others are spurs jingling, their eyes a buffalo stampede. Me? I'm just an ole Alabama boy watching them all through the binoculars of my prose.

YOU have had THEM and I have had THEM? Those golden key moments when our very lives change on the spin of a dime.

I'm almost embarrassed to tell you one of mine. I was 18 and had thumbed to California from Alabama. Yes, I was "California Dreaming" and my chief ambitions were to develop one of the most outstanding physiques in all of America and to own a Corvette convertible. The TV series, Route 66, had kidnapped my mind and heart.

I ended up working as an instructor at an old Vic Tanny gym in Long Beach near the ocean, where an amusement park aroused children of all ages. Hear the adults SCREAM on the rollercoaster.

The ride I rode working in the gym was hardly as thrilling, for it was only part time and a corvette demanded far more pennies than my short stack. I was living with my cousin and his wife and a friend of his had a "position" at a factory in Burbank, where the workers assembled and tested metal hoses for airplanes and jets.

I took a job there and found a room in a boarding house, where an elderly Jewish man in the gathering room daily sat at a table creating mosaics, as if trying to glue his broken life together. He was as alone as I was.

Two weeks into my new full time job at the hose hustling factory, the man working next to me confessed.

"When I retire I'm moving back home to Kentucky and buy me a little farm. Get some cattle and chickens. A couple of horses."

That was the very moment, from the ceiling of my life that a Corvette crashed, knocking some sense into my hard "California Dreaming" head. The man dreaming of that Old Kentucky Home was only in his early forties and had twenty more years of fitting one hose into another before being putout, in his fantasy pasture. The sadness in his voice even while savoring a sweet distant dream was, thank God, more than I could bare.

I took the first Greyhound Bus I could grab and was dropped off in the desert away from LA's cluttered and honking traffic so I could thumb back home to Alabama and feed myself like a starved hog at the trough of higher education at the University of Alabama.

I have a secret (well, many actually) that I will only share with YOU. Right before I go to bed each night, I not only behold the splendor of the moon; I reach up and grasp it between my thumb and index finger, where in my very private world it becomes a treasured pearl of blue or whatever color my soul desires. The moon humors me and plays along, as I place it under my pillow. Sometimes in the night, it rolls around on my chest and then comes to a stop over my gently beating heart. For a few seconds, I believe I am part of the mysterious universe.

When I awake at dawn and behold the fiery sun, I come back to Earth humbled that I am but a man, one with the moon's footprints on his chest. I show these tracks to very few and most always say the same, "Oh, my, if others only knew!"

San Francisco and its Coit Tower became major landmarks in my wandering journey. SHE was tall and slender with red hair and I met her at Zim's, a famous restaurant chain for the rich as well as for the humble.

BEFORE I met HER, I had talked at the Zim's counter with a Frenchman who sculptured marble into classic designs of beautiful women. He and I CLICKED and dived head and heart into what we at least believed was at the center of the Human Condition. After an hour of setting our mental woods on fire, he shot me a wry grin to bring us both down to Earth: "And as Voltaire said 'It is NOW time to pay the bill.'" The two coffees didn't cost a heap, but let's move on to that slender red-head, so beautiful and sensual that after I met her at Zim's I phoned where she worked. Her tone was both welcoming and a bit startled.

"How did you get my number?" she said.

"You told me where you worked," I said. "Phone books have stores to tell. You really fascinate me and may I have the pleasure of seeing you again?"

She lived on Russian Hill overlooking Coit Tower and the cable car couldn't run the night I walked toward her flat. A lightning storm had swallowed the electric grid. Her historic high rise was as dark as some people's souls and just how I would find her flat in such blackness was beyond me.

Still, by faint moonlight, I found her building, and I stood in the dark lobby, the fire in my heart and loins light for ME but NOT the inner building

THEN, like a mythological creature, a LIGHT appeared as a candle dancing as she descended the long steep spiraling staircase. Step by slow step, like an Edgar Allen Poe story, the candle light grew brighter as she grew closer. She was a firefly signaling her magical arrival.

"Hello," I breathed in and out the fire.

"Hello," said the firefly. "Glad you made it in this darkness."

"That was one hell of a storm," I said.

"Come into my harbor," she led us up and UP the spiraling staircase to her flat that offered a balcony overlooking Coit Tower. There we stood becoming acquainted over a glass of white wine, and an hour later the cable car chimed as the lights came back on and she and I rang each other's bell in the Edgar Allen Poe night. Quote the Raven: She had once been a nun in Wyoming but lost her Faith to become as Holy as Flesh.

I was an aspiring writer living in New Orleans and often visited in the French Quarter the parked streetcar named DESIRE, the name crucial in Tennessee Williams' famous play, A Streetcar Named Desire. I had had two one-plays produced but they were but baby teeth gnawing yet on the toes of success.

I waited tables in the International Hotel on Canal Street, and the woman from San Francisco I served intrigued me. I invited her after work to have a coffee at Cafe Du Monde. Her Jewish ancestors had fled Russia to the USA around 1900 during a certain Revolution and she, Dianne, had just graduated from a California law school and had passed the bar examine. Before she started her promising career, she had the foresight to reward herself a car trip across America, her very own country that she had never seen. Me? I had seen the great USA, warts, jewels, and all several times for a whole decade as I thumbed almost non-stop from New York to San Francisco, and Oklahoma City to Mexico City, staying in OKC with a friend, Dan, who had been my Creative Writing teacher in graduate school. Never mind too much right now that he was close friends with the famous poet, e.e. Cummings and drove the widow to the poet's funeral. They had met one summer when Dan attended graduate school at Yale, though Dan grew up as poor as the Grapes of Wrath, the son of a windblown mule trader in Tuttle, Oklahoma.

Dan and Carole and I became as close as three peas in a pod and all lived a few blocks from each other in OKC. I had married Carole in 1970, after thumbing five times from the University of Alabama to OKC to see her, spending a single sweaty lust-driven Saturday night with her, my leaving on Sunday morning to arrive back in Alabama in time to attend my first class of Shakespeare. "To be or NOT to be?" never was my question for I believed heart and soul and young flesh that I WAS BEING to the sky and back.

Dianne, from SF, was yet years away but don't worry, you and I are circling the wagons to get back to HER. Carole became head of PR for the Oklahoma State Library, and on a trip to a conference in Houston, she fell for a man who had an MIT degree and worked pulling strings for NASA to play with the starry, starry nights.

A full-blooded Cherokee in my Creative Writing Class with Dan, the instructor, was an attorney who had become my friend and offered to do the divorce papers for 50 bucks He and I went to the elderly judge's little office and my confessional was less than earthshaking, I guess, because after two minutes the judge fell asleep. My Indian attorney gently tapped the judge's shoulder and the old man, not much older than me today, came back from the dead and followed the Indian's pointed finger to sign the ADIOS papers. Carole got the new car and all the furniture and I got all the money we had saved, a startling heap of two grand, plenty of money for me to HIT THE ROAD for a whole decade before I ended up as a great writer, writing down mere food orders at the New Orleans International Hotel.

The second night that Dianne, staying in that hotel, and I left the building to hit the French Quarter after I shed my soiled waiter clothes, she invited me to jump ship and leave with her the next day headed to New York and Quebec. It was so totally impulsive and RIGHT that I leaped at the Adventure, she and I staying often with her Jewish relatives along the way she had never met before.

Each night, she and I in bed took turns reading parts of the book, Wind in the Willows, to each other, which was near perfect our own Grand Adventure--LIFE.

In New England, Dianne had started carving a pine block of wood the size of a caring hand.

"What are you making?" I had asked one night along the way.

"Something," she said. "If it turns out I'll show you."

When she and I parted company is Colorado, as we had planned when we left New Orleans, she presented me with the wooden carving, the replica of an 18th Century New England candleholder. On the bottom of the candleholder, she had carved, "With Love. Not perfect, love nonetheless."

"We will always be friends," she said.

"HOW do you know that?" I was gentle.

"Because somethings a woman just knows."

Decades later, Dianne is still a close and cherished friend, and she even came down from SF to Carmel to have lunch with Debi and me. She ended up staying several days as if love of one becomes love of two, a candle we might all pray burns eternally.

"Toad, with no one to check his statements or to criticize in an unfriendly spirit, rather let himself go. Indeed, much that he related belonged more properly to the category of what-might-have-happened-had-I-only-thought-of-it-in-time-instead-of-ten-minutes-afterwards. Those are always the best and raciest adventures; and why should they not be truly ours, as much as the somewhat inadequate things that really come off?" Wind in the Willows.

You MIGHT wonder how a dragonfly brought me a GIFT today and it's something beyond my usual Spiritual Bond with Nature, all its majestic beauties.( I don't deny tornados flipping giant trees onto houses to kill our fellow Human Beings or the destruction of floods, sweeping cherished property and human

bodies and cats and dogs into HELL. See that lawn chair and

ripped red shirt in a treetop?)

I went to the creek today to one of my favorite ancient

Native American village sites, where the Indians didn't simply

manufacture tools, weapons and stone Art. It was also a trading

post because of so MANY treasures dating back thousands of years

up to European contact to offer trading items, both of glass and

metal, to the Indians in exchange for pelts and beeswax and, man

being what he is, likely sex. Let's be REAL, right?

I Believe in SIGNS from Nature, as I behold the crane, my

Spirit Bird, crows and insects, when I "hunt." Hey, my hunter-

gatherer DNA is strong. But what about that dragonfly?

I had just arrived at the creek and a dragonfly circled me. It

was as green as my eyes. The dragonfly then landed on a rock a

foot from the clear spring-fed water. I looked closely around him

and then in the water, carrying on its ancient flow. I spotted

nothing out the ordinary and the dragonfly as if dropping sun-golden breadcrumbs, flew two feet to land on another rock closer to the mystical water.

I took a step and THERE, there IT was. An artifact, a stone chisel. I lifted it from the creek and water dripped from it, the dragonfly lifting from the rock to disappear into the Mystic. BELIEVE, my dear Brothers and Sisters, in the Magic of Life, the Mercy of the Great Mystery, for there is Medicine for your Soul and Body.

When I was five, we lived in an Alabama sharecropper's house, owned by my Melungeon/Native American aunt, and my parents paid 25 bucks monthly for rent. We had no indoor plumbing and I was afraid at night to go to the outhouse. My older sister, Sandra Ellis Lafferty, now an acclaimed film actor, slept with my sister. Sandra told our younger sister, Nita, that the owl hooting in the night was a Witch coming to get her so that Nita would hug her. She still needs hugs, but then who doesn't?

Debi, my late beloved wife and soulmate, INSISTED on doing ALL of the designing and carpentry in her music studio. I don't often go there now, for the ghosts yet haunt it, just as our love yet lifts me in Tanager House. May I tell YOU a guarded secret? Days before she died at home, her eyes pulled me to her bedside:

"When I am gone continue to do the things that make Jerry JERRY," she struggled to breathe.

I took her hand.

"How will I know if you reach out to me from the Other Side?"

She tried to touch my face but she didn't have the strength.

"Look for me in the creeks," she whispered.


"Two monks are on a LONG pilgrimage and come upon a man beaten in a ditch. Trying to save the man, one of the monks secures a strong bond with the injured man, who dies. They bury him and continue the JOURNEY. The one who had the big bond with the buried man has trouble keeping up with the first monk, who turns and says gently, "Brother, why are you carrying a dead man?"

San Francisco, like human hearts and minds, holds so many surprises. I first arrived in this magical city by thumbing there from Alabama, around 1975, to behold the Golden Gate Bridge and hear one of the infamous cable cars ring its unforgettable bell.

My younger sister had a flat in the city and Nita welcomed my visit, my extended stay. Her flat was on the third floor and at the back of the building was a rusty iron fire escape ladder. It overlooked an avocado tree, heavy with the fruit, and towered forty feet toward flying seagulls, calling out both day and night.

On the tiny balcony of the fire escape ladder rested a ten-foot bamboo with a hook, made from a coat hanger, attached to one end of the bamboo.

"Spread your jacket wider," she called down from the balcony to me who stood on the ground. When she and I were children, we believed like many children that if you spotted a little private plane in the sky that those aboard the flight would actually

obey when you shouted with your heart, "Drop me some candy!"

"I'm ready," I shouted up to Nita, the bamboo in her hands.

"Don't drop any," she called down.

"How many can you reach?" I eyed the dozens and dozens

of tempting lush avocados, ripe for the picking.

"We'll find out," she said.

"Drop me some candy," I held my jacket wide as if I might

catch a wayward fairy who had lost hope, ready to leap from life's

ledge.

She snaked the long bamboo into the tree and one by one

pulled ten ripe avocados free to fall into my welcoming arms.

While she and I had not returned to the Garden of Eden, we had

certainly revisited the MAGIC of our childhood. The avocados

were, of course, the "best" we ever ate and to this day, decades

later, I sometimes spot a plane in the sky and callout, "Drop me

some candy." And you know WHAT? Sometimes, candy falls

from the sky, even if many people can't see it.

I rarely quote people. But many years ago the famous choreographer, Tommy Tune, the hottest director on Broadway, appeared on the Tom Snyder Show. His wise words took root in my soul.

Tom: "It must be very difficult to arrange so many complex and varied dances on stage?"

Tune: "Not once you get the FEELING. Then it's simply a matter of craft. Of execution."

AND this is True for everything I write of any value.


When my sister, Sandra, and I met for three hours with the director, John Behring, who had flown to Atlanta from LA to discuss making a movie from my book about walking the Trail of Tears, we had lunch outdoors. John was yet hurting because several months earlier he had lost both his mother and his uncle to the Virus.

Once he released some of his hurt through conversation, I said, "May I move your coffee cup and silverware?"

I sat a Medicine Bundle, the size of two hands joined, of red cloth tied with a strip of white tanned leather, where the cup had been. I untied it making sure he couldn't see what the bundle contained, and I, one by one, handed John the items.

"Because we are all broken," I gave him an ancient Native American pottery shard. "That by the end of our movie many in the audience will feel WHOLE. At least for a while."

I handed John a pink-white arrowhead, "That our aim is true and honorable."

His eyes were softening, his big heart opening wider.

"Homegrown tobacco," I said, "to give gratitude to our ancestors in the Other World."

I lifted the next item from the Medicine Bundle.

"A strip of the canvas sweat lodge I used at the end the Trail," I said. "That our film will set a fire like the one in the lodge that might brighten the world."

I saved the biggest item for last. I handed him the green bird-shaped stone pipe I had carved.

"That we will one day," I said, "smoke this together for our prayers to rise UP to the Great Mystery giving gratitude for helping us get this movie made."

The look on John's face was a Medicine Bundle for me.


You just never KNOW, do you? Not until you ask, anyway. Yesterday at the local big grocery store called Foodland, I was in the Less Than Ten Items Lane, and a short, wiry, elder was the only customer in front of me. He was brown, as if he likely had some Cherokee or Creek blood flowing in his aging veins. A big wad of tobacco swelled his cheek. He wore a John Deere cap. When we made eye contact, he hooked me.

"How are you?" I said. He studied me, surprised, it seemed, that I would ask.

He moved the tobacco to the other side of his mouth. "I ain't bragging none," he sniffed. His clothes were wrinkled but clean. His eyes were so beautiful, so tender, so sad, so dignified.

"No, sir? Something wrong?"

"I'm supposed to always wear oxygen," he said. "Guess I did a few things I should not have done but that tank weighs thirty pounds." He adjusted his cap. "I left it in the truck."

"How old are you, sir?" I smiled.

"Eighty-one," he said as if reading a number from a phone book or a late bill.

I touched his small shoulder. "You're looking good."

"Doctor says I have about nine more years."

"All the way to ninety!" I gently placed my arm around his shoulders. "You stick around, hear? We need you."

The cashier handed him his small plastic bag.

"Not sure ANYBODY needs me anymore," he said.

"Why I needed you to talk to just NOW," I said.

His grin was as subtle but as endearing as a lightning bug's flicker in distant dark woods. While he may have returned to a tank that weighed thirty pounds, the Oxygen he gave me took fifty pounds off my back. When I stepped outside, I beheld lush Lookout Mountain and took a breath. A DEEP breath. It was a good moment in eternity to be alive.

Debi's grandfather was friends with Clint Eastwood in Carmel, and both were mayors of the little seaside village. My wife and I lived there for three months and would visit SF from time to time.

Before I met Debi, however, I was the road bum you now know and around 1975, when I came to SF for the first time and stayed with my sister on Larkin Street, I was modeling at the SF Academy of Art.

I often took Bart to Berkley and continued on a bus to the coffee houses on Telegraph Avenue seeking most of all myself, under the guise of speaking with fascinating strangers, material for my writing and food for my hungry soul.

One day on the bus, a tall slender girl boarded the bus and sat beside me. SOMETHING jingled in her large bag and I asked, "What is THAT?"

Our eyes were comfortable with each other and she opened the bag. "I'm just returning from the city where I take belly dancing lessons."

She lifted a string of golden bells that rang my heart.

I told her about my life on the road and she came along as if we were old-new friends. Enchantment in her eyes, she lowered her pretty head, long black hair flowing, and offered, "I could dance for you if you want?"

"Really?" It was the most beautiful, sensual and poetic gift anyone had ever offered me. "You'd do that for me?"

I went home with her. Her flat, on a hill overlooking Berkley, was perfect for a college student. A blue parachute bellowed from the ceiling as if the sky itself floated above us. She struck a match and the tiny yellow flame set afire a stick of incense.

"Make yourself comfortable," she said, "and I'll be back in a few minutes."

She disappeared into her bedroom as the sweet fragrance of sandalwood filled the room, the blue sky yet slowly falling. I soon heard Middle Eastern music like MAGIC coming from her bedroom. I envisioned giant tents in a windblown desert, where camels gathered and a man rode a white horse with a leather-hooded flacon perched on his majestic shoulder.

My new friend loomed almost naked into the living room to dance as golden bells dangled from her agile and beckoning fingers.

Every move of her hands, arms and legs were in perfect timing with the exotic music and she danced without a worry in the world, her dark Jewish eyes sometimes peeking into mine. Her sensual sweat became honey with her long black hair.

I was under her spell and when long minutes later she stopped dancing she sat on a chair across from me, breathing heavily, searching my eyes, waiting for me to toss golden coins of kisses minted in a stranger's desire and admiration.

I reached into my pocket and dug through the pennies of my road life to find riches that she and I then shared as strangers sometimes do when the soft blue sky falls upon them, little by little, to carry them entwined to the heart of the Milky Way.

When I was fifteen, I walked for hours in woods I had never before explored. Ten feet above the earth, I beheld a fox, a nocturnal creature, curled up on oak knot as big as an elephant's head.

The fox looked into my eyes, steady and strong. I did the same with him. Why was he about in sunlight? Was he like me, a misfit? I took a step on the autumn red and gold leaves and thought he would leap to the ground and race into the mysterious unknown.

YET, he stayed still, save for his head slowly shifting an inch as if stalking me, my very soul. I stopped. He and I seemed to come closer. I took another step forward and his eyes bored into mine. I eased on, his beautiful eyes owning MY eyes.

For about ten minutes, as I progressed, he and I were in touch in a way I had never before communed with another creature. Once I had passed him, I turned back to find him still watching, as if he guarded me, trying to tell me something my young mind could not, at the time, phantom. I didn't understand how he did it, but he became part of me that day and I yet see his gentle caring eyes probing my own mystery.

Many years earlier, when I tagged along with my father and three other hunters in deep woods we didn't see a fox. But when a blue heron appeared over the treetops one of the men shot it from the magical blue sky.

Tiny blue feathers floated over the gold and red leaves as the crane crashed to earth, and the man who had killed it jerked a knife from his pocket and cut a wing from the bird to smile as he stuffed it into his hunting jacket.

My father and the others hiked on but I lingered over the dead bird to kneel and stroke its smooth back. I became startled, when a single eye opened to stare as if even from death it lived, trying to tell me something.

When you and I meet in person, if you look closely you will perceive in one of my eyes the fox and in the other eye the blue heron. Somewhere between the two, you will discover the man I have become. In turn, I will call upon the Medicine given to me by the fox and the fallen crane to SEE you, who you really are behind your masks, masks that we all wear to contend with life's pains and sorrows.

Once in New York on the subway, I beheld a young man with a dozen red roses. He gave them, one by one, to elders on the train, such joy filling their faces, as if no one had noticed them in a long time. That stayed with me, and today I gave a gold bell to the young cashier, Emma said her nametag, at Foodland. She stood six feet tall with thick curly black hair cascading to her shoulders. Her perfume smelled so good, like a discreet whiff of sandalwood in the air. Her eyes, for some reason, inspired me to imagine a blue parachute floating softly from the magical sky, and for a second I thought I heard Middle Eastern music playing in the exotic distance.

Emma eyed the gold bell in her hand, her eyes brightening.

"I'll dangle it from my rearview car mirror," she smiled.

"I happened to have the bell in my pocket," I said, "because this week I carved a stone pipe for a friend who had commissioned it and I attached a bell to the pipe stem with feathers. Just so you know I don't usually walk around with bells in my pocket. Just on my shoes."

She played, "On the tip of your shoes?"

"Only when I dance," I winked. I danced from Foodland richer than when I had entered.


Richard wasn't your average Marine, but then again what Marine is or ever was "average." When I was 17, I gave serious thought to enlisting, thought I was a bad ass from the Great State of Alabama, but I went the Way of the Open Road. But, HERE, this is not about ME, but my Brother in Spirit, Richard.

I met him in a New York bar, The Riviera Cafe, in the Village the day before I was to return to Alabama. Over the bar bottles, a life-size woman, an Art piece, swung from a trapeze. Richard and I, sitting beside each other at the long wooden counter, had both had enough to drink to swing with the trapeze Artist.

We clicked in a New York minute and he sent his son, about 10, to run home to bring a secret.

Justin returned with a leather briefcase. Richard set it on the bar and opened it.

"Pick the one you like the most," he said.

The case filled with rare daguerreotypes, and I had just told him the past hour of my fascination with photography. When he returned from Vietnam, LOOK MAGAZINE asked him to return there to photograph men in combat.

"I've seen all the killing I can stomach," Richard told LIFE. "I'll go back and photograph the children there." His son was half-Vietnamese.

Richard honored his word and his photos featured in LIFE, the magazine giving its first and only editorial salute to a photographer. Richard's book, Warriors, was nominated for a Pulitzer Prize, his powerful images capturing Marines at boot camp at Paris Island.

The next ten years, I went often to NYC and I always stayed with Richard, who stood almost 6 foot 6 in his boots. His strong gait alerted people on the sidewalk to clear the way. A proud Marine was marching on. To get to the Riviera Cafe. To swing on that trapeze.

Driving to Alabama to visit me for the first time, he was with his Chinese girlfriend when he died of a heart attack. Did I mention that he ALWAYS sent his Vet's disability check to his struggling mother in Pittsburg? I salute you, Brother Richard, for being a Marine and for loving me as if we were blood. Yes, sir, I still have the daguerreotype you gave me, as well as the many photos I took of YOU. Rest well, friend. I miss and love you and am forever grateful for your kindness.

It's hard to know for certain just WHY the Great Mystery sometimes leads me to extraordinary people, and that happened yet again yesterday in a large Fort Payne grocery. Perhaps it happens, at least in part, because I pray daily to find Magic and Wonder in this often cruel world, that I might "pass it on" as a writer.

The man, about my age, caught my attention as I rolled my silver squeaky shopping cart, called a "buggy" here in the Deep South. He stood tall with a radiant complexion as he leaned against the freezer with the organic frozen food I sought. His presumed wife, only six feet away, placed other items in her "buggy" and the man appeared impatient but not to the point of tugging on his wife's blouse. Not YET, anyway. I had no idea, of course, who I was about to meet. I just knew his face intrigued me and I sometimes find intrigue to be the spark that starts a fire.

"I like your cap," I said to him. He smiled to reveal beautiful teeth below gentle eyes.

"Thanks," he said. Never mind that he didn't comment on my black broad rimmed-hat with a ten-inch crow feather sticking from the leather band. I didn't seek a fashion critique, just a way to open the door to his inner home as he leaned against the freezer.

"You a deer hunter?" I tried to insert a golden key into his door.

"Oh, no, I'm a duck hunter," he smiled.

Most Southern folks like to be messed with and if one does it with heart people take it a sign of warmth so I said: "How's the duck killing these days?"

His grin was subtle.

"Not good," he said. "Last year I didn't get a single bird."

"Really? What's the problem?" I remembered the day the man had shot the blue heron from the sky and cutoff its wing as a thropy.

"Their flyways are changing," he said. "Like over on the Tennessee River farmers are planting fields that used to be swampy and the birds are staying there to eat instead of moving on. Some hunters shoot at ducks too high to hit just to say they have shot at some and I don't go along with that."

"Pretty good news for the ammo companies," I half-smiled.

He grunted and his door opened wider, inviting me in. "I also hunt deer and wild turkeys." Hocus-pocus, a minute ago, he wasn't a deer hunter but NOW he has become one.

"Better luck there than with those high flying ducks?" I said.

He tone was modest. "I let a lot of deer go free," he said. "But I killed ten last year. I only kill what I eat, but give most of the meat to friends in need. I like to have my meat made into sausage mixed with hot peppers."

"Oh, brother," I opened his door wider, "I love spicy food." THEN, somehow, I felt the presence of the Great Medicine Ghost, where I didn't "speak in tongues" but spoke from my gut-heart.

"You part Cherokee, sir?"

He chuckled and his hand pushed my question away like a spider web you and I both have felt brush our faces as we have walked in the summer woods.

"Oh, no," he chuckled yet again as he yet leaned against the freezer, his wife having rolled on out of sight. We were two ole Southern boys shooting not ducks or deer but shooting the shit. "I'm from up in Tennessee near the Hiawassee River. My great great-grandfather was Cherokee with hair to his shoulders. He was the only Cherokee general during the Civil War."

The door was almost fully open now and I just HAD to really mess with him a lot now that I had taken a seat in his house.

"So you ARE part Cherokee," I said. "You ashamed of your heritage?"

He didn't chuckle THIS time. He laughed freely as I leaned back in my chair in his inviting home.

"No," he said. "That grandfather helped lead a group of the Cherokee to Oklahoma on the Trail of Tears." I had said nothing about my connection to the Trail or my own heritage.

"I'm guessing your grandfather's name was Stan Waite?" He looked at me as if 100 ducks had just flown from the produce department of red cabbages and yellow squash and landed at our feet. "I have a particular interest in the Cherokee," I said. The 100 ducks at our feet quacked as if they were begging for it.

"Honey," his wife called out, "I'm ready when you are." The puzzled man had reached a crossroads right there leaning against the freezer, torn between his wife and those 100 ducks.

He chose his wife and I could get the frozen food. When I checked out, I carried my three plastic bags from the store followed by a flock of ducks and that magical look on the man's face led to the perfect flying V.


I AM AMERICA!
I am Native American and was here before Europeans arrived
My ancestral father was a Viking
I have been a thief of human emotions

I have given away all I owned to those in need

I have lied, sinned, denied others my love

I have dropped to my trembling knees and begged the Holy

Ghost for Forgiveness

I AM AMERICA

I have wandered lost and weary without a map to land or soul

I have slept with more women than you dare wish to know

I have loved with ALL my heart, given mercy when others smirked

I have been staggered drunk falling to the hard streets

I have crawled seeking a crack to hide myself

I have lifted myself by Grace of the Holy Ghost to walk the

Trail of Tears

I have become rich in Spirit and Gold

I AM AMERICA

I have traveled the world and speak other languages

I am so ignorant that I lower my head in Humility

I have given into ego and spoken too loudly

I have sat as quietly as a mountain to listen to mice squeak

I have learned that I am nothing and that I am everything

I AM AMERICA

I am a poet

I am man who can barely utter a meaningful word

I cook exotic meals for others to show my love and gratitude

I have gone hungry without a penny to my name

I have questioned if I am sane

I am brilliant

I inspire

I see my Death before me, the threads of my life a golden rope

That pulls ever forward as my ship keeps coming in

I AM AMERICA

I fight a war like a hero you can not see and yet know it is your

war as well

I shake strangers' hands just to feel their skin, their spirit

I am as weak as the broken link in the chain

I am the skyscraper so towering that you gawk

I am the ant inside the earth you never see

I am the Council Oak where you come for shade

I AM AMERICA and so are YOU!

Be Proud, Be Bold, Dare others, Love with all your heart,

Stand tall as the stars

Know you are forever as small as the egg that your Mother gave

you and Honor your Father as if he were sent from the Holy

Ghost!

WE ARE AMERICA


In the Old Days, the Cherokee placed black walnut hulls in

woven sacks to place in creeks to numb fish just enough for them

to float to the water's surface for easy picking for food. Even my father, born 1913, practiced this old tradition on Sand Mountain in the Old Cherokee Nation, when he was a boy determined to find enough food to keep him alive. Now every time a walnut falls from one of the autumn trees at the base of my wooded hill I smell fish frying, my father happy and eating well on the Other Side.

The rollercoaster saga of my broken car, twisting and turning like a bat out of hell, flies onward. A few weeks ago, my car broke down twice in two days, and the last time was Easter at the gas pump of the Mapco in Fort Payne. Two rednecks, beautiful as Angels, helped me push it from the gas pumps.

I hightailed it to the cashier and described the big bump in the road.

"I can call AAA now," I said. "Or may I leave it here overnight because I hate to bother a tow truck driver on Easter Sunday?"

She looked out the window where my car perched like a bird with two broken wings.

"It's fine until tomorrow," she promised. "Just put a note on the windshield."

"Mighty kind of you," I was grateful. "I'll be here with the AAA tow truck by eight in the morning. My mechanic is just one block away."

I try always to honor my word and was there before eight the next morning. My car was gone.

Another cashier worked the morning shift. "Ma'am," I said softly, "no offense to YOU it's just that my car is GONE and I was assured it was safe to leave it here overnight."

"I think I know what happened," she picked up the phone and learned that my car towed into the Great Unknown.

I arrived at the tow truck company, the very one that works for AAA, and I had met both drivers before. They broke into my locked car to stir it to pull onto the tow truck.

"It's $100 to get it back," the male driver said.

"My number was on the note," I said. "Why didn't you call me?"

He pointed at the other driver. "She did."

"I get robo calls around the clock," I said. "No text to confirm who you were?" She just grinned.

"We text people all the time," said the man, "and they never answer."

"I know basic math," I said, "and would have put 2 and 2 together."

"We're not charging you a storage fee," he looked away, as if guilt whistled.

"Your generosity is killing me," I said. "Please tell me you didn't wash and wax my car?"

I slapped a 100-dollar bill on the desk and called AAA. "Where is the car now?" said the sweet voice.

"At the tow truck company you use," I said.

The truck pulled my car to my mechanic across the street from where I had left it at trustworthy Mapco.

Later that day, I got an email from AAA: "Were you pleased with our service today?"

We live in such a funny world. I'm sure I will die laughing my ass off. Yet, he who laughs last laughs the loudest. In two weeks, a dear friend is giving me a car coming from California.

We never know, for sure, when and where a door to childhood will open. I was around 6, when my father in the woods said to me, "This plant can talk."

"WHAT?" I said.

He touched the tiny fern-like leaves of a vine with nickel-sized pink sphere flowers. When his fingers brushed the leaves, they folded as if to eat the air. I went 65 years without seeing that plant again until a few days ago. It was still talking to my father as its leaves folded. It's the cats' claw brier, that is also called shame boy. The talking vine with its beautiful pink flowers grew from the edge of the shaded woods into the ditch along my dirt driveway as if to look for me. It's so reassuring to be found and especially in a world where so many people get lost.

As one ages, his/her thirst for Knowledge accelerates at the speed of Light, perhaps in preparation for the fast approaching endless Night.

Sometimes, if not OFTEN, it is a struggle for Humans to escape their many worries, but we must forever reach UP, to whatever you believe, even if it is yourself only, for otherwise we wander through life with a big bag of rocks draping our shoulders. To swim through life's many floods we must leave that bag of stones on the doorstep of the Past, for the Present waits for neither woman nor man to transform rocks into a boat.

There will be days, even when the ancient sun glows brightly and the infinite sky blue promises HOPE, that we shall feel that the only friend we have is our shadows upon the earth. We MUST hold our weary heads high until our shadows merge not only with our flesh and bones but with our hearts, for in reuniting ourselves we will again feel whole and complete to meet even total strangers as ourselves, with fascination and kindness.

There are those who THINK about doing something, those who do it without thinking, and those of us who wonder, what the hell was I thinking when I did it?

Life is more fun with delicious surprises, don't you think? Here's a Cherokee recipe for Fried Green Tomatoes. Who is having me over for lunch?

Ingredients:

2 lbs. Green tomatoes

4 eggs

1 1/4 cup Corn meal

3/4 cup Water

1/4 cup Minced chives or wild onions

1 Tbsp. Salt

1/4 tsp. Pepper, fresh ground

1/4 cup Butter or margarine

Directions

Slice the tomatoes 1/2" thick, but do not peel or core. Drain well between several paper towels until most of the moisture of the tomatoes is absorbed.

While the tomatoes are draining, make a batter by beating the eggs until light, then mix in the corn meal, water, minced chives, salt, and pepper. In a large, heavy iron skillet, heat the butter or margarine until bubbly. Dip the tomato slices into the batter, and brown on both sides. Serve immediately.

We have spun a unique web on social media. We are a community of jokers, deep thinkers, sellers (Hey, why are you looking at me like that?), common folks who, of course, are NOT common, Artists of various kinds, people who rant and rave, beg for prayers, and certainly the occasional troll. We reveal our true selves more than some might grasp. In Native American cosmology, the spider web represents the human condition. Touch a single strand of the web and the WHOLE web feels it, vibrations sometimes going far, wide and deep. You and I make that rare web shake by our posted words and images. Some people are careful and wise where they step.

This spring here in the Old Cherokee Nation, I feel flowers blooming inside my soul. Not sure, but I THINK an oak is taking root in my heart. I'm certain a spring bubbles in my Spirit. Here, have a drink from that spring. Let's sit for a while and trade stories as blue jays land on our shoulders.

When I moved from Fort Payne, Alabama to Hollywood in 1985, I slept on the floor of my cracker box flat, until I found a mattress in the alley. It was heaven to have a bed, as I sought to make it as a screenwriter. One of my scripts was about a man who walked the Trail of Tears to redeem his soul and honor his Cherokee ancestors, raising awareness about their plight, 4,000 meeting DEATH on the forced march from the Deep South to Indian Territory in 1838. Sometimes, I reflect on that mattress. It was not only where I rested from my endured days of failure, it was where I dreamed, my soul leading me to awareness that I had drawn a map for myself: I was the man in the script that had to walk the Trail.

Even a tiny spark from your soul to another is worthy in this sometimes dark world. Don't hide your LIGHT. Some people need gentle encouragement. Others need a hard kick in the ass. By themselves.

I'm SOAKED TO the bone as I walk through a storm down a country road in western Arkansas. I don't mind the wind and rain so much, but I'm scared to death of lightning. If a bridge or bam were in sight, I'd run for shelter. But forget it. There's just me and trees, swaying in the wind. For the first time in my life, I imagine how a mouse might feel the moment he looks up to see a hawk shoot from the sky to drive claws into his tiny heart.

I wear a hat; a black crow feather sticks from it, while a rattlesnake rattler with eight buttons rides snug under the band at the back of my head. Jeans cover my aching legs.

Lightning flashes yellow once again, as if to see if I'll try to run under a rock. I'm tempted.

The road is flooded and small waterfalls shoot from the rock banks. My feet are blistered and on my back is a red and blue backpack weighing fifty pounds. I've walked one hundred miles in six days and I have eight hundred more miles and seven states to go. I promised myself I'd walk the whole way. But have I lied?

I'm forty-one now, but when I was four years old my house was struck by lightning. I was home with my mother and two sisters and we smelled smoke coming from the attic. I was sure the house would disappear in flames and we'd have nowhere to live. My father, a carpenter, came home from work minutes later. He climbed into the attic with a bucket of water and threw it onto the fire. That put out the flames, but he slipped and fell through the ceiling. He crashed atop a piano and onto the floor. I learned then and there that lightning, as beautiful as it is, doesn't give a damn about man.

I walk facing traffic and a truck, hauling horses, roars toward me. The driver leans forward and squints in disbelief. A cigarette dangles from his mouth and he becomes a blur behind windshield wipers.

As the truck shoots past me I'm hit with a blast of wind and water; for a split second I can't see. My hand flies to my hat to grab it just as it jumps from my head. The snake rattler shakes and the smell of horses pierces my wet nose.

The lightning is much closer now, and I recall hiding behind a big chair in the comer of my house during a thunderstorm when I was in the fourth grade. A bolt of fire might get me, I reasoned, but it would have to find me first.

Boom! The thunder follows and a car stops. It's a station wagon with the front fender falling apart with rust. The back is loaded with lumber, plastic pipes, and a garden hose coiled like the snake from whom I got the rattler.

The driver motions for me to hop inside, but I hesitate. A little girl with a candy bar— there's chocolate on her chin—is propped against his shoulder. A Band-Aid is stretched across her temple. The driver rolls down his window.

Get in, he shouts.

The little girl smiles and it's so cozy and dry inside. Water runs down my nose.

I can't, I say. I'm walking the Trail of Tears.


"Your hat makes me think of an old man I used to see when I was a boy," says Bud, a Georgia historian, as I walk the route of Sherman's March to the Sea from Atlanta to Savannah. "His hat held little things he had found on the side of the road. He traveled all over America in a wagon pulled by goats."

"You mean Goat Man?"

"You've seen him?"

"Several times when I was growing up. You're the second person who's mentioned him since I left Atlanta. He was a kind of folk hero to me. I wish I could have talked with him man-to-man before he died."

"He's not dead. Not unless he passed on recently. Last I heard, just a few months ago, he was still alive and kicking down in a Macon nursing home. He has a young girlfriend there. She's in her eighties."

In *A Streetcar Named Desire,* Tennessee Williams's Blanche says that she has "always depended on the kindness of strangers." I can't deny that I, too, must often thank strangers for guiding me down the right path. I'll walk to that Macon nursing home, meet my childhood folk hero, and see just what he and other elders there recall about the Civil War. Why, he might even be inspired to come out of retirement and straddle a goat alongside me.

It is a hot, exhausting two-day walk from Milledgeville to Macon. But after I get a motel room and shower I feel refreshed and excited to see the Goat Man. I visit the public library to research him. His real name is Charlie "Ches" McCartney, and he's followed the twists and turns of more roads and had more lovers than I dared dream of.

Born in 1901 near What Cheer, Iowa, the Goat Man was often bullied by other kids because he didn't act like they did and was branded a misfit. At the age of fourteen he ran away to New York City where he married a twenty-four-year-old Spanish knife thrower. They scratched out a living in bars and pubs where the Goat Man worked as her target. The closer she stuck the long silver knives to his head, the better their tips were. He filed the blades daily to make certain they'd stick in the wood so she wouldn't have to repeat a throw to appease the boozed- up audience.

"Those were the *easy* days," the Goat Man tells me after I arrive at the Eastview Nursing Home, a modern brick building a few miles east of downtown Macon, where he's been since 1988. "After I divorced the knife thrower I went back to Iowa and wrestled at county fairs to make money. One day I took on a black bear."

"A bear?"

"I wanted to back out. But two men pulled me by my hair onto the platform. I spit bear hair from my mouth for two days. I beat him only because I was so scared and God Almighty took mercy on me."

The Goat Man rubs his left elbow, which is deformed with a knot as big as a lemon. We're sitting in the lobby of the nursing home and I'm totally entranced by this gentleman who is now ninety-two years old. This living legend has a strong and yet gentle presence, and he connects me to my Southern roots in a way no one else can.

I first met the Goat Man when I was nine years old. My older sister, Sandra, came home and told me that the Goat Man and his son were camped just down the road by a creek. I had never seen the Goat Man before, but I had heard that he looked like a mountain man with a long beard and he slept with his goats on winter nights to keep him warm. He could speak Goat and understood everything his animals said. If he wanted, he could turn himself into a goat and hide from people. He lived mostly on goat milk, but he could also turn plain old field rocks into delicious soup simply by dropping them into a pot of boiling water and stirring them with the same staff he used to drive his herd. He knew many other secrets, too, but wouldn't tell anybody unless they gave him food and he liked them a lot.

I sneaked through the woods toward the creek and heard the goats calling out long before I saw them. There I spotted the Goat Man with his long beard and overalls. He was bending to place a car tire on a fire, and then he stood, bigger than life itself, surrounded by thick black smoke. I looked for his son, but saw no one except him and some fifteen goats. Had he turned the son into a goat? Atop two small wagons were signs reading: Jesus Wept and God Is Not Dead. His clothes were covered with buttons, whistles, tinfoil, cigar wrappers, Coke and RC bottle caps, pencils, and even a spark plug dangled from a string tied around his neck. Getting a close look at him, I wasn't so sure that I wanted to sample any of his homemade rock soup. But my curiosity was heating up to fever pitch.

"What are you doing out there, boy?" he called, and I would've run back home right then but I was too frightened.

"I brought you something, Goat Man."

"Come out where I can see you better."

My heart was pounding as I stepped from the woods and held up a brown paper sack.

"Don't be afraid," he said. "Children are the joy of God, and I mean no harm to anyone. What do you have there?"

"Something to eat," I said, eyeing him, the goats, and the wagons as if they might vanish before my very eyes. The metal wheels on the wagons had no rubber, and pots, pans, signs, cans, buckets, gourds, birdhouses, mirrors, hubcaps, wire, and more were tied to the wagons' sides and tops as if the Goat Man ran a traveling junk store. I was still uneasy, but when he stepped closer I could see into his eyes. They were warm and kind and I offered him the bag. When he bent over to take it, the spark plug, tied to the string around his neck, dangled forward and rocked back and forth like a pendulum to an old clock. Around eight of his fingers strings were tied. I figured he had so many secrets that they were there to remind him.

"My mother made it," I said, after his fingers gripped the paper sack.

He reached inside the bag and pulled out a big piece of peanut brittle. My uncle had raised the peanuts and my grandfather had raised the cane for the molasses that went into the candy. The Goat Man took a bite and nodded. I was sure I had won his favor and he would now tell me one of his secrets. But Nita appeared from the woods.

"Mother said for you to get home right now," she called out, "or she's going to whip your behind with a hickory switch."

It was rare that my mother ever lifted a finger against us, but I had sneaked off from the house and I didn't want her to worry. Then, too, Daddy would be home any minute from work and one of his main rules was that his children be there when he arrived so that we could all sit down together at the dinner table. He didn't tie string around our fingers to remind us, but a lick or two from his leather belt had an effect on my memory.

"Will you be here tomorrow?" I asked the Goat Man.

"Only the morning light knows that," the Goat Man told me. "I might not be alive tomorrow."

I told him I hoped he stayed and that I'd come back, but early the next morning as I brushed my teeth to prepare for school I heard the musical rattle of the wagons and the eerie cries of the goats as they passed in front of our house. I ran to the front porch and waved as the Goat Man and his son—he hadn't been turned into a goat after all—disappeared down the road with the animals and a secret I feared that was lost forever.

"I know a story about Sherman," shouts an old woman hobbling forward as she braces herself with a metal walker. "It's more interesting than anything that old goat will tell you." "She can't help it," the Goat Man says. "It's human environment. That's all it is, human environment. She wants attention."

*"Well,"* the old woman snaps again, "do you want to hear my story or not?"

Gossip about my journey has spread through the nursing home as fast as a wildfire and I'm both touched and a bit put off by this bundle of nerves who shakes her witchy finger as she speaks.

"What's your name?" I ask.

"Helen," she says, her tone softening.

"I do want to hear your story," I say, "but it would be better if we waited till I've finished talking to Mr. McCartney." "You don't have to lie to me," she yells. "If you don't want to hear my story, just say so. I've been lied to before and survived. If you think goats know more than people, then just go right ahead and keep fooling yourself. It's no gravy from my bowl. I can still hootchy-kootchy like I did sixty years ago." Helen, in her eighties, begins to shake her whole body while she holds on to the aluminum-frame walker, and eight or ten others in wheelchairs or with canes begin to gather, a couple of them clapping their hands. One elderly gentleman has black skin, red hair, and a growth on his forehead about the size of a grape; it's purplish-blue. The bizarreness, how-ever, is overshadowed by a radiant innocence in his face. And on his lips is one of the most curious little grins I've ever seen. It may be only wishful thinking on my part, but he seems to find everything amusing as if he had learned long ago from a mirror that humor was his salvation. Judging, too, by how calm the Goat

Man is staying during this outbreak of celebrity envy, he's experienced it more than once and has learned to sit it out with grace.

"How do I look?" Helen shouts, her shoulders rocking back and forth faster by the heartbeat as her narrow hips try to keep the beat.

"You need to be in Las Vegas," says an old man in a wheelchair. "You're hot."

"I think it's disgusting," says an old woman leaning against her cane. "A lady shouldn't carry on that way."

"Human environment," says the Goat Man as he shakes his head. "Human environment, that's all it is. She means no harm."

"I never made it to Vegas," shouts Helen, "but I was a main attraction in a carnival for over three years. Madam Hoochicoochi they called me, and my picture was as big as an elephant on the side of a truck. Let's see you shake like this, Goat Man. You can't do it, can you?"

More and more of the old folks are arriving by the second and I'm trying to decide what to do when Joyce, who operates the nursing home hair salon, dashes from her little room down the hall to take Helen by the arm.

"Oh," Joyce says, "if I could dance like you I'd never cut hair another day to make a living. If I could do even half as well, I'd be pleased with myself. Won't you finally please show me some of your steps?"

"You really care?" Helen says.

"I do," Joyce says. "I care about anything you want to talk about."

"That man back there don't." She points at me. "I got a Civil War story but he won't listen."

"I met him earlier," says Joyce. "I think he's just so interested that he wants to have you all to himself later."

They disappear into her salon and she closes the door. The others begin to go about their business and I turn to find the Goat Man holding a copy of *USA Today* rolled up within six inches of his eyes; his lips move as he reads.

"Mr. McCartney?"

He lowers the newspaper and I once again behold his wondrous, kind eyes. Only two teeth remain in his aging head.

"I'm sorry we were interrupted," I say. "You were telling me how you hurt your arm?"

"I was working for the WPA," he says. "A tree fell on me. It's just nature's way. When I was found several hours later, I was out cold with my arm twisted and broken. They took me to the morgue and started to stick me to drain my blood, when I woke up. God had sent an angel to rub my eyes."

Unable to do much work now that his left arm was ruined, and refusing to go on welfare, the Goat Man decided to explore America. Inspired by Robinson Crusoe, he persuaded his new wife to make him, her, and their son, Albert Gene, goatskin clothes in which to greet those they met along the roads they traveled. Averaging twelve miles per day with his goat caravan, he supported himself by selling postcards of himself and his family with the goats. Everywhere he camped people flocked around him to scratch their heads and perhaps wish they were as free as this prophet, poet, and self-made gypsy king.

"Most people were good to me," says the Goat Man, "and some brought me food and money. But more than once I was beat up and hit over the head at night. Sometimes people threw bottles at me from their cars or trucks. They turned my wagons over at night."

In 1941, the Goat Man and his son moved to Jeffersonville some thirty miles east of Macon on Highway 80. In addition to the money he made from the postcards, he received donations from those who heard him preach. His church was usually the shade of a tree and he encouraged men to love each other and try to overcome their greed. Hundreds of spiritual signs nailed to oaks and pines throughout the Deep South were his handiwork, and they proclaimed God Is Kindness and Jesus Is Your Friend. When he and his goats wandered into the isolated mountains of north Georgia, some living there claimed that the Goat Man was Jesus Himself.

"I never said I was," says the Goat Man. "But when they decided I wasn't, they tarred and feathered me. I was a hell of a mess. Down in south Georgia in World War Two people thought I was a Nazi spy and the sheriff searched my wagons. He didn't find a shortwave radio because there wasn't one. People can't help being weak and suspicious. It's just human environment."

He finally built a little church of his own with a dirt floor in Jeffersonville and called it the Free Thinking Mission. It doubled as his home, but burned to the ground in 1978. He and his son then bought a school bus and lived in it near the church site. That was ten years after the Goat Man stopped traveling with his caravan. Back in 1968, on Signal Mountain near Chattanooga, Tennessee, he was mugged and the wound on his head required twenty-seven stitches. The same thug slashed the throats of eight goats. Days later, headed to home sweet home, the Goat Man awoke in Conyers, Georgia, to find two more of his goats had vanished. Rumor said one was barbecued. The second had been tied to the railroad tracks and departed Georgia with the early morning train.

"I just never had the heart to keep going with my goats after that," the Goat Man tells me. "But I didn't stop traveling. I just started walking and hitchhiking."

Indeed, he didn't stop. When he reached his eighties, he thumbed all the way from Macon to Los Angeles. Already the ex-husband to at least five wives—the Lord works in mysterious ways—the Goat Man had a crush on the starlet Morgan Fairchild. Bound and determined to marry her and bring her back to live in Dixie, the Goat Man found himself in an L.A. hospital after being beaten and robbed of his U.S. savings bonds. He flew home to

Albert Gene, who was still living in the parked yellow school bus.

In forty years the Goat Man and his billies wandered across forty-nine states and Canada.

"I would've gone to Hawaii," says the Goat Man, "but my goats couldn't swim. Anyway, if we'd made it they would've just eaten the grass skirts off the hula dancers."

His eyes get big when he speaks of those grass skirts being eaten away and I love the fire that still heats this old man. At the age of ninety-two, he has more passion for living than some folks in their twenties. And as I sit here beside him, rubbing his aching and deformed left arm where the tree fell on him, I feel as though I have completed a kind of circle and come home in some rare and special way. Almost forty years ago I gave him some candy in hopes of getting one of his secrets, but he disappeared down the road. Life's true secrets are, of course, found in the sum of our experiences, and for thirty years now I've been on the road learning those secrets through the joy, sadness, thrill, intrigue, and reflection of those I have met. I'll never know how much this now-delicate old man influenced me to follow the life I've been leading, but I suspect it's a great deal. How blessed I feel to behold his living legend, one of my roots still feeding from his spring.

The Open Road is NOT for everyone, just the strong and restless, so in love with life that they can't help themselves.

It is wiser to eat an apple from the muddy ground than to wait with your mouth open for the "perfect" piece of fruit to fall from the tree.

Joy, Kentucky, is so small, that next to it Golconda, Illinois could pass as Swinging Sin City. It's here that I meet Beverly Crittenden, eighty-two years old, sitting outside her garage with her dear friends, Sweet Talker and Pretty Thing, two ten-year-old roosters.

The pack too heavy to carry all the way up here? she snaps.

I let the pack ease onto the ground near the Trail. I like that she has challenge in her bones.

Well, I say. I didn't want to bring it to the house first thing. I was afraid you might see my plan to move in with you.

She's an old woman, but her eyes are as sharp and alert as those of a twenty-five year old. It's also clear that she's watching my eyes to see what I'm made of. A self-proclaimed old-maid, she taught school fifteen years and then decided money was more fun than kids; she became a banker till she retired. That garden spot down there? Yeah, she plows it, plants it, and picks it.

I canned 342 jars this summer, she says. Why shouldn't I? If you slow down too much, you dry up and blow away. But you were asking me about Mantle Rock. I played there when I was a little girl. Found lots of artifacts too. A couple of years ago, the last time I was down there—back before my leg went out on me— my heart just broke. Somebody had gone in there at night with a bulldozer and unearthed the Cherokee graves. And for what? They didn't have anything when they passed through here.

Why do you call the rooster Sweet Talker? I say.

Because that's what he does, Beverly snaps. He gives me pretty songs.

You mean he crows? I say.

Now, you know that's not what I mean, she says. You heard him crow already. He sings too. You want to see?

Her right leg is lame and her brace broke a few days ago. She comes from her chair and must walk on her right ankle to reach for Sweet Talker. He walks backwards because, according to Beverly, he was pecked too much when he was a chick. She finally talks him into her hands and lifts him as if he's part of the Greatest Show on Earth.

Show him, she whispers. Show him how you can sing. Go on, don't be afraid. Yes, my precious Sweet Talker. Such a pretty bird. Won't you sing for me? Come on—she whispers ever more softly—you show him how you can sing such pretty songs.

As if understanding the old woman, the rooster finally begins to make a delicate clucking sound. It's no nightingale, but the way she holds him and looks at him creates the rarest of songs. Within her private dreams he seems to fly her way beyond her wrinkles and crippled leg and I guess it's true that we get love wherever we can find it.

You want to see my canned goods? says Beverly, lowering Sweet Talker to the ground.

We go inside and she opens the door to the cellar. She refuses to let me help her as she must go backwards down the stairs just like Sweet Talker did on the ground when she first tried to catch him.

If Sweet Talker is her best friend, then these towering shelves of canned fruits, vegetables, jellies, and jams are her children. Standing next to them, but sure not to block any of them, she is a prideful queen.

You're a regular canning factory, I say.

We go back upstairs and she shows me the relics she found at Mantle Rock when she was a child. They're some of the best spearheads I've ever seen. I'm so involved with examining them that she finally takes them from me and closes the drawer where she keeps them. I take the gesture as a hint to leave, but when I say as much she begins to drag out old bottles and fans—anything that's old and unusual, to hold my attention. For the first time, when I again tell her I must go, she drops her mask.

I don't get to talk to many people, she says.

THE KENTUCKY COUNTRYSIDE is alive with rolling hills and barn lofts, hanging thick with tobacco plants turned upside down to cure as small, steady fires burn on the ground to keep moisture away. Smoke rises from the barns' tin roofs to fill the evening air with aromatic tease.

The night's beauty becomes stronger when the orange harvest moon rises atop a hay field and the smell of the smoke blends with the cool moist air. Except for an occasional light in a distant farmhouse, there's no sign of human life. It seems as though the moon shines for me and me alone. This is no longer a walk. I have gone beyond the point of no return into an odyssey. Maybe it happened before tonight and I simply wasn't aware of it. Like falling in love, maybe such a thing happens little by little, till a man is over the edge. In any event, I have, for at least this phase of my life, found my form. The middle-aged crisis, if that's what it ever was, is passing. I don't understand it, but I am no longer afraid of dying. Perhaps it's simply because I am doing exactly what I want to and feel good about it that makes me whole. Still, as happened just a few days ago when everything was so solid, I'm hit with a gnawing anxiety. What happens when the odyssey ends? What do I do next to keep life this fulfilling and exciting?

Something is off, or different, tonight that I can't yet put my finger on. I've been walking for over an hour in the moonlight and find what I think is a good place to camp in a field near a grove of oaks. An owl hoots nearby and it seems safe here. But once I begin unpacking the tent, I get the feeling I should move on. I obey and head down the Trail for another mile or so.

I begin to pitch the tent again and the feeling returns. Not a single time before tonight have I unpacked my tent and not camped where my feet marked the spot.

But I once more repack the tent and walk on through the moonlight. This is no big deal, but I'm not sure what's going on with my instincts—if that's what it is—to keep me moving. Am I going away from something or toward something in the night? In any event, I find a third spot and this one is just right. I crawl into the tent, take off my clothes, and slide into the sleeping bag. I'm atop grass eight to ten inches thick and the bed is wonderfully soft. The moon shines through the nylon and my little net window to make a perfect home.

My body and mind begin to dissolve into one with the moon, smoke from the barns, the day's journey across the great Ohio River, the buck, turkeys, Mantle Rock, and of course, Beverly with her Sweet Talker and cellar kingdom of fruits and vegetables. Then I see myself walking the Trail to Mantle Rock; I feel where I squatted in the shadows, the sky another world up there beyond the trees. Then I experience something I have never known before:

I begin either to fall asleep or step further into the odyssey that now owns me. My chest feels as if it is no longer skin and bones, but a delicate membrane which opens, not unlike a tender mouth about to kiss, and into it comes a floating tribe of marching Indians made of pale blue lights. Startled, to say the least, I rise from the grass bed with the belief that such a thing—surely mere images so close to the conscious mind that they couldn't wait for deep sleep to play—will fade instantly and I will again have at least the illusion that I am in control of my life. But the faint blue luminous figures, mostly children, do not cooperate with my reflex logic. As gently as the smoke rises from the barns' exotic leaves, they continue to walk floating into my chest, into my heart. I have only the moon to console me and its harvest light seems concerned with the sole purpose of empowering the ghosts or spirits or whatever they are to march forward into my both frightened and transfixed being. It all lasts only a few seconds— oh, doesn't time make some changes on an odyssey—but before they vanish I have the merciful opportunity to be both involved and outside the rare event in the same breath. Not unlike an orgasm, but in this case a spiritual one, I feel its beginning and know I can only go with it, though it seems of another world or another dimension.

I am left sitting up as if awaiting an explanation. I tell myself that they were simply a flash dream that lingered. I had fallen asleep without realizing it. Everything on the journey has become so magnified that this is only another example of man's ability— and need—to enrich his trace of existence. I'm not just a man. I'm a part of God, with magical and mystical powers. I won't die and simply become dust. I will live forever. But even a loner, priding himself on individuality, will sometimes try to direct himself back toward the herd if he feels he is wandering too far away from accepted reality.

But, no, even if I am far, far away from the crowd, I won't lie to myself here and now. I made contact with them, or something, in a realm as real as the earth to which we all return. They are in me now. They are part of my soul.

Bless the man and woman who, in humility, lower to their knees to pray. But rise up with he who has learned that the Great Mystery is most pleased by the ultimate Prayer--ACTION!

KINDNESS to others is the LOVE you give to yourself.

"WHY do you write?" someone once asked me.
I answered, "Because my heart beats."

Words spoken in anger become the razor blades you eat.

Digesting them rips your guts open.

After lunch, the wagon train rolls down a dirt road on the Oregon Trail, leaving behind the old Indian mission and the children waving good-bye. They fade into the distance, but I'm haunted by their screams when the stampede occurred. David has cleaned the mud from his clothes and face, but his aged eyes still look uneasy from the day's tumble down the hill.

That evening, when we arrive at the night's campsite in a lot next to a football field, I find a young man with a chubby face coming my way.

Are you Jerry? he grins.

Yes, I say, shaking his hand.

I'm Larry. We spoke on the phone last night. I've come to take you to meet Ernest.

The gleam in his eyes makes me feel like there's a real treat in store for me in this mysterious Rabbit Man of Kansas. We crawl into Larry's truck and start for Troy, which is some thirty miles back to the southeast.

Have you known Ernest for long? I ask.

Oh, yes, my whole life.

He really lives in a hole?

Yes. Larry giggles like he did last night when we talked on the phone.

You take care of him?

Oh, no, says Larry. He takes care of himself. I just take groceries to him. I've been doing it for years. He makes out a list each week and puts it in an envelope with a stamp and my address on it. The mailman picks it up, marks through the stamp with a pen, and drives down the dirt road to my mailbox about a mile away. It's always the same list, more or less.

That's kind of you to take him groceries.

It doesn't take long. I have a lot of spare time.

What do you do for a living? I ask.

I work at a feed mill three days a week. I did work every day, but things have dropped off the past year.

He slows his truck and we roll up another dirt road toward an old barn, hay sticking out from the loft. Chickens are running around and scratching the ground as they cackle. Larry stops the truck and we get out to face a banged-up and rusty old trailer house. I'm disappointed that Ernest may be fudging on the truth and live here some. I want a full-time Rabbit Man.

Does he live in the trailer sometimes? I ask, wary of the answer.

He wouldn't think of doing that, Larry explains. This is just where he keeps his animal feed and a deep freeze for his ice cream. The door's cracked a little, so he's probably in there now. He's expecting us.

Larry knocks on the trailer door. It swings open to one of the strangest-looking people I've ever seen.

Ernest appears to be in his seventies and he hasn't shaved in a week or two. He wears two pairs of coveralls with the knees worn from the first pair to reveal the second, red pair underneath. He's as dirty as a coal miner, but his eyes beam with warm, life-giving curiosity. He has no teeth within his big smile and he leans on two canes. One is a store-bought cane. The other was cut from the limb of a tree; his fingers rest in its Y.

Good to meet you, he says, extending his hand like any fine and caring gentleman. I'm so happy you came to see me. Would you like an Eskimo Pie?

Not just yet, I say, still staring at this kind, homely stranger.

Five or six kittens meow and crawl over his dirty, heavy shoes.

He continues to stand in the doorway, and on the wall behind him is a tempting calendar from the fifties: a pinup girl with long, smooth legs descending from short shorts, while her big breasts are peeking from inside a dangerously revealing halter top. It takes me several seconds to realize that she holds a spark plug with a tiny yellow flame blazing from it. She's either advertising car parts or she has human electricity for sale or rent.

That's some girlfriend you got there, I say.

Ernest leans on the tree limb cane with the Y as he turns to study the calendar beauty. He laughs as if I don't know the half of it.

Yep, he says. She's a sweet one.

Where's the hole you live in? I say, feeling only a moment later that I may have been too forward too fast because Ernest gives me a funny look.

We'll head that way now, Ernest offers.

The kittens run from his giant shoes and the sensual gal in the calendar disappears behind the closed door as Ernest hobbles down from the trailer. He uses two canes with ease as we wander over to an old shed where a 1930 Chevrolet is parked. It's covered with dust, and boxes, boards, wire and tin have been piled on the hood.

My daddy bought that car new, recalls the Rabbit Man. He's dead and it doesn't run anymore. This airplane in the other shed over here was built in 1946. I was flying her myself till just a few years ago. I could land her right out there in that field. Well, it's grown up some now.

I look to Larry to confirm the truth. He nods that Ernest is, indeed, a pilot, whether he has a license or not. I like this whimsical little Rabbit Man and his old plane covered in as much trash as the 1930 Chevrolet. I almost expect him to suggest that we pull it from the mess and take it for a flight, his canes sticking out the window to shake at Troy as we buzz the little police station.

I miss flying that old plane, Ernest confesses. But sometimes I have two friends who come by and I go with them to model airplane meetings. I get all cleaned up when I do that. Sometimes I put on a tie.

I try not to stare, but his face is such a wonder to behold because of all the joy in it that it's difficult not to.

Up here is what's left of the house I lived in before I moved into the hole, he says. My mother and daddy built it back in the

1880s. It burned to the ground except for this rock foundation. But I know, you want to see the hole. We're almost there. Just a little farther up the path.

Why do you live in a hole? I ask him.

I don't have to worry about tornadoes, he says with the convincing clarity of a hole salesman. It's also easy to heat. When the house burned, I just got a pick and shovel and starting digging.

I live part time in a cabin, I say, that started out as a giant tree house.

A tree house? he grins, pausing on the path and leaning on his canes. I always wanted one.

We walk past some bushes and an apple tree green with new leaves. A small shed—which looks like it might collapse if we sneeze—has a tin roof over a wooden trapdoor. Ernest lifts it to reveal his hole-home, going straight down into the sweet earth. It's as dark as the tunnel of love.

Want to come see? invites the Rabbit Man. I'll go down first.

The Rabbit Man eases down into the hole with his canes and disappears into the darkness. When I begin to do the same, Larry giggles and his big belly shakes.

Have you been down there? I ask.

No, says Larry, and I don't plan on it either.

No, comes the voice of Ernest from the earth, Larry never comes into my home.

When I ease down into the hole, the Rabbit Man lowers the trapdoor. We're in total darkness except for a few rays from the setting sun coming through a dirty skylight. My eyes begin to adjust and I see that the room is barely big enough for us and a potbellied stove where he burns wood for heat and cooking. I like the smell of the damp earth as I strike a match. The flame shows the Rabbit Man's proud smile.

Where's your bed? 1 wonder aloud.

You're standing on it, says Ernest without judgment.

I discover that I'm standing on a pile of flattened cardboard boxes. Then the match goes out.

Sorry about standing on your bed.

No harm done, he says. 1 walk on the boxes all the time. I sleep just fine. It's cozy and warm down here when it snows a foot deep *up there.*

Ernest reminds me of Jimmy Stewart in the movie *Harvey,*

which is about a six-foot rabbit most people can't see. Both Ernest and Jimmy Stewart's character seem to accept life as it comes while others get in a hurry and bent out of shape.

I like your hole, I say, trying to eye his impish face in the dark. It makes me feel good.

I'm glad you like it, says the Rabbit Man. I couldn't live any other way now.

I wish I had brought my backpack, I say. I'd pitch my tent here on your farm, if that was okay. I'd like to get to know you.

That's a good idea. Can't you go get your pack and come back?

I'm with a wagon train. It leaves in the morning.

Oh, that's too bad.

You want to leave the hole first? I say.

No, insists the Rabbit Man. After you.

I crawl out of the hole to find Larry still grinning as when I descended into the little earthy home. Ernest soon struggles back to the surface with his canes.

Twilight is falling over the rolling hills, the barn and the sheds housing the 1946 plane and 1930 Chevrolet, as we retrace the narrow path by the foundation of the burned house. I'm a bit torn about leaving this wonderful old man. I feel relaxed and at peace here. This is a most welcomed change from the tensions on the wagon train and the violence at the Indian mission today.

When we arrive at the trailer, Ernest opens its door. His eyes beam with new hope.

How about a Milky Way? Will you eat a Milky Way with me now?

Could I have it for later? I say. Then, when I eat it, I'll think of you.

Ernest laughs as he pulls a frozen Milky Way from the freezer, the sensual calendar girl staring at us from the wall, forever ready with America's best spark plug. I put the cold candy bar into my pocket.

Thank you for showing me your home.

I hope you'll come back someday, he says, leaning on his canes. Maybe next time you can stay for a while and have an Eskimo Pie.

Ernest is so warm, gentle, and simple that I almost feel like giving him a hug as I leave. He certainly has given me one whether he knows it or not.



Say, mister, says a huge cowboy on a horse, in Wyoming on a
ranch where I helped brand cattle as I retraced the Pony Express
Trail. He hurried toward me to ride alongside. I sure am sorry I
almost trampled you earlier today. My horse don't usually spook
like that. He must've gotten a good look at my old ugly face.

No harm done, I say, thinking he's kind to mention it. It let me
know I can still run when I have to.

You can sure jump, too, mister, he grins. I thought for a second
you'd jump right out of your skin.

You worked on this ranch long? I say, becoming more amused.

He uses a pocketknife to cut a piece of tobacco and slide it into
his mouth. His cheek bulges as he closes the knife blade and drops
it into his pocket.

I don't work here at all, he says, almost choking as he tries to
chew the piece of tobacco. I live down in Texas. I just come up
once a year to help out for a few days because I like to see my
friends here and look at these mountains. I don't know, it just

somehow fills me up and makes me feel young again ever time I do it. I guess it's just something you're born with.

He offers one of the most beautiful and innocent smiles I've seen on this journey, and tobacco juice drips down the corner of his mouth. It's almost run to his chin when he rubs it on his sleeve.

It washes out, he says with an apologetic tone.

He then grins, nods, and kicks his horse with his spurs to make it race toward two other cowboys on horses some fifty yards ahead of us. As the horses' hooves rise and fall, they sling dust into the Wyoming wind, and I imagine for a few glorious and magical moments that they are the hooves of a horse ridden by a Pony rider back in 1860.

When the tobacco-chewing cowboy slows his horse to join his two friends, I look to my right to discover the slender woman with the shades and the pink cap. She rides her horse with such smoothness and grace that she seems to float through the air. When we arrive at The Buzzard and gather around the tables to eat dinner, she takes a chair across from me.

Mind if I sit here? she asks, setting down her shades and removing her cap. Her long hair falls over her shoulders.

No, I say, liking her clear and curious eyes. Please do.

What I really want to do is pick your brain.

Why *mine*? I say, feeling flattered but put on the spot.

You're a writer, aren't you? I wondered what you write.

People and places, I say. Thoughts and feelings. Things that happen along the Trail.

The two worlds, says the cowgirl. The internal world and the external world.

You must be a writer yourself, I say, or want to be?

I can't express myself very well. I try to put down what I feel inside sometimes. I write poems sometimes about being a woman, a mother, a cowgirl.

The cowboy next to her pokes her with his elbow.

Tell him who you are, he says.

Oh, she says, lowering her head. You just shut up.

Who are you? I ask, my curiosity building.

I'm sorry. My name is Tanya Stevenson.

She's a world champion bareback bronc rider, the cowboy tells me.

No, says Tanya. It's nothing. I love to read, but my husband,

Otie, doesn't like for me to. He thinks it's a waste of time.

Wait a second. You're a champion bronc rider?

Bulls, too, says the cowboy. She could ride a tornado.

I won the Women's Professional Rodeo Bareback Championship in 1979, 1980, and 1989. In 1979 and 1980 I won the Bull Riding Championship. My mother, Jan Yowen, who helped me brand today, is also a champion bull rider. Look what you're doing. You're getting into my brain instead of me getting into yours.

I'm a better listener than I am a talker, I say.

Bob, my host for the night, sits to my right while his wife, Tammy, sits next to him. Whatever the caution was I saw in her face when we met has vanished. She eyes me with warmth and openness. I feel just a bit naked when I discover that the entire table of some ten people has stopped talking to listen to Tanya and me. We are the pin heard hitting the floor.

You know what Tanya said about Otie not wanting her to read? says Bob. I feel the same the same way when Tammy reads. Except I don't think it's a waste of time. I just want the attention instead of the book getting it.

I admire your honesty, I tell Bob.

Yeah, laughs one of the cowboys, but he's more interesting when he tells a big lie.

Tanya's husband—he wears white feathers in his cowboy hat—turns thirty-six today and a birthday cake with a candle atop it is now placed on the table. Otie is blowing out that tiny flame when the ranch boss hurries into the room. He carries a ten-year-old girl in his arms. Her head hangs and her blond hair dangles toward the floor.

My God, says a woman hurrying to her feet. What happened?

The horse got me, Mama, says the little girl.

They were playing in the barn, says the ranch boss.

I'm sick, Mama, says the girl. My stomach hurts.

The girl is placed on a couch near the tables. Her mother puts a washcloth on her head and I'm concerned that the stomachache signals a possible concussion. But the nearest doctor is sixty miles away in Casper and nothing is said about him. One of the older cowboys goes over to the girl and sits on the edge of the couch. He puts his hand to the washcloth on the frightened child's head.

Well, I'll tell you, honey, he says, we all get knocked around and stepped on a little in life. But we get back up and keep going, don't we?

Yes, says the girl. That's what Daddy says.

Yes, that's what we do, says the old cowboy. We get back up and go on.

I still can't help but worry that the girl has been injured more seriously than anyone is saying.

Don't worry, Tanya tells me. She'll be okay. I'm a mother, and kids can take more knocks than we think possible.

Tanya takes me to the barn where the girl was trampled. It's here that she stores some of the saddles she won riding broncs and bulls. In her house, across from the barn, she shows me her gold and silver medals housed between the spokes of an antique wagon wheel that now serves as a coffee table with a glass top. Now that we are alone Tanya's face and eyes have taken on some new light, as if she's happy for us to have a few minutes away from the others. I guess most of us have a need to meet new people in new places with different thoughts than our own and imagine what it would be like to live like they do. I'm happy again to recall that I can come and go as I like along the Trail.

When Tanya and I come from her house, I spot Bob and Tammy standing by their truck and I head their way.

You looking for me? I say.

Yeah, says Bob, we're ready to leave.

Is the girl feeling better? I ask Tammy.

Yes, says Tammy, and so is her mother.

I climb into the truck with Bob and Tammy and we drive away from The Buzzard. As I watch Tanya wave good-bye, I look at her strong hand, a hand that sometimes holds a pen, sometimes a wild bronc. I feel drawn to her, a woman unafraid of even the poetry in her heart.


I consider myself a hip and aware person, but I am often humbled to discover I am sometimes BLIND. I have the past few months traveled my 300 yard-long driveway hundreds of times. Yesterday, as I drove home from the grocery store I was thinking I need to add some Queen Anne's Lace to Debi's memorial garden. I planned to find some and dig up the roots this fall to transplant them. THEN, coming up my wooded dirt drive I beheld a beautiful lone bunch of the Queen Herself blooming. HOW had I not seen them before? Debi, did you place the Queen there, your lovely royal hand reaching from the Other Side?

On Father's Day, many of you will reflect on your fathers and I find myself doing the same. Daddy grew up on Sand Mountain in NE Alabama and his mother died when he was only three. When he and his father and many brothers and sisters traveled in a horse-drawn wagon to his aunt's burial, they returned home to find the house burned to the ground.

Like other poor families, they survived by eating from their gardens, fishing and hunting. When he was a boy, he once gathered with his cousins in the night to light a pine knot to light their way along Town Creek, where they used tree branches to knock many birds from the brush, before they roasted them on the ends of sticks like their Indian ancestors once did over campfires.

A quail hunter, he and I once walked a frozen field with bird dogs leading the way. I had no gloves and shivered. "Give me your gun for awhile, son," he said. "Warm your hands."

A carpenter, he brought home scrap lumber and bent nails from his worksites, and he straightened the nails on an iron anvil at the barn, the same barn where he built a saltbox to cure hams.

Muddy and sweaty and just home from work one evening, he said: "Don't end up being a carpenter, son. Try to make something of yourself."

He was smart and a champion at all three major sports, his index finger broken while playing catcher at baseball. He didn't go to a doctor--money was scarce--and the finger healed crooked. When he was hurt deep inside his angry finger dug into my chest to get his point across. When I was five, I threw a hunting knife that pierced my older cousin's cheek just beneath his beautiful eyes. Daddy jerked his leather belt free and whipped me until I curled into a ball and retreated to the floorboard of our old car to hide my tears and shame.

In the thick Alabama woods, he once carved me a foot-long knife from a poplar limb. It was Magic, somehow, and could kill monsters unseen. Before he dropped dead in our garden as he planted whip-poor-will peas, he got to see that Magical knife mysteriously transform into a writing pen. He only read TWO

books in his whole life: The Call of the Wild and a book about

some guy who walked the Trail of Tears, which he read twice.

At the funeral home, I placed a Medicine Pouch in his wrinkled

hands. It contained shavings from an oak staff. Whip-poor-will

peas and secret sacred items, which I believed were for his Journey

to the Other Side. The Medicine Pouch, in reflection however, was

for me to continue my Earthly journey to honor my father, his grit,

determination, and caring love.

He always kissed my mother when he left for work, his tin

lunch box in his hand with ELLIS painted on the side of the box.

When I was a boy, he always kissed my cheek goodnight.

He sometimes retreated to the barn with the saltbox built from

white oak and there on a table he had made, he placed walnuts on a

flat stone to crush them with a rock. I would sneak upon him

unseen just to hear him make up songs that came from his hurting

and happy soul.

I still have that wooden knife you made me, Daddy. THANK

YOU for all you taught me, the values your pointed crooked finger drilled into me. Maybe we'll meet again one day and feast on whip-poor-will peas as I kiss your cheek on the Other Side. I love you.

Once I found a tree, I climbed it to escape the masses. I could still HEAR them, and some shook the trunk.

It's cool to be cool, but not so cool that we become cold to the world. Let your heart melt often. It waters the thirsty Soul.

My chain saw died and boy did I have fun downing a 40-foot white oak with a handsaw. I cut it near where I will raise my new giant owl's nesting box some twenty feet into the air. The chosen spot is 30 yards into the woods beyond Debi's memorial garden and when owls might nest in it I will hear them hoot, WHO? WHO? I will know, of course, that the answer is, "Debi calling out from the Other Side."

Everything is Relative, isn't it? I was walking in Missouri and an Amish family in a horse-drawn carriage pulled up beside me.

"That pack looks heavy," said the man in his hat, leather reins in his hands. His horse eyed me. His wife and three children gawked. "Why are you out here walking, are you homeless?"

"I'm walking HOME to Alabama," I said. "I'm on the Trail of Tears."

He squinted, intrigued. "That's a long walk."

"Why don't you get a car or truck?" I interviewed him.

"Cars go to fast," he said. "We don't want to be pulled into the corruption of the modern world." He eyed the pack, sweat dripping from my hot cheeks. "You want to ride with us?"

"I can't," I said, "you go too fast and it might corrupt me."

The expression in his bright eyes was worth a million bucks, which I deposited in my heart, as I walked on into the unknown.

We're all such fragile threads but what a tapestry we make.

I love to add to people's happiness. Do you recall my story several about my giving a gold bell to the cashier at Foodland? She happened to be my cashier again this morning.

When I placed my gallon of water on the counter, she said, "I have my bell. I placed it with some pottery my dad made. It's a special place."

"I put YOU in a special place as well," I said. Her eyes widened. "I'm an author and the exchange we had about the bell days ago is in my ninth book called Breaking Bread With Misfits."

"REALLY? I'm in a BOOK?"

"Yes, you're in two places at once. You're HERE and in a BOOK."

I THINK she heard two gold bells ringing, if her eyes were the wondrous wind that swayed those chimes. Live FREE. Be BOLD! LOVE like there is no tonight.


Dear readers, I hope this book has added to YOUR happiness and thank YOU for becoming part of my tapestry by joining me on this journey in Breaking Bread With Misfits. Some of what you read you already forgot and some will likely linger within your heart and mind for untold time to come. We never know, for certain, just what will stick with us, do we?

Then, seemingly out the mysterious unknown, images, feelings, and thoughts of the past present themselves like little treasures. With all my heart, I hope such treasures will help you in your hours of sorrow and self-doubt, that they might offer even morsels of spiritual food for your soul.

A book breathes life by word of mouth so I am grateful if you will offer this book to others as a gift. Time is so precious and I'm fully aware your life is busy, but I respectfully request that you leave a review of Breaking Bread at Amazon. Maybe one day you and I will meet in person that we might break warm bread together and rejoice in every bite.